T0302220

Praise for Say What?! Communicate with Tact and Impact

"You're going to need more than one highlighter for this one. Tons of great advice and stories."

Trent Russell, Founder, Greenskies Analytics

"Ann Butera's latest book will empower anyone in an assurance role to take action quickly with confidence based on clearly-written advice. I am excited to share it with my colleagues!"

Mary Lochner, Internal Audit Finance & Operations at Accenture

"Ann Butera delivers a power packed practical guide for any internal audit or compliance professional desiring to build credibility and gain trust. Take to heart the lessons and skills Ann shares and you will deliver results that get attention and positively impact your organization."

Michelle Piranio, Chief Audit and Compliance Officer

"Ann's book has a message for everyone whether you are interested in developing, strengthening, or refreshing your communications skills. It is a practical and easy to follow road map for communicating with tact and impact and effectively managing conflict. A recommended read for internal auditors, risk managers, info security, and anyone working in an assurance-related position."

Audley Bell, Retired Chief Audit Executive, World Vision International, and Audit Committee Chair, Wingate University

"The art of successfully influencing others has been a challenge for leaders in every age. In a virtually connected world, Ann's effective communication methodology and nuanced tactics guide the reader to adjust his or her individual approach as needed, an essential skill."

Martha Jane Gagnon, Senior Associate Audit Director

"Ann's book provides real world practical approaches that help auditors, and other governance and risk professionals drive transformation."

Felix Vargas, Head Group Internal Audit – Americas

"It's real, it's personable, and it's not a stuffy textbook that's going to put you to sleep…and that's rare for Audit! It grabs the reader's attention with bold statements and proclamations that are innately insightful and thought-provoking."

Matthew Cesaro, AVP, Internal Audit

SAY WHAT!? COMMUNICATE WITH TACT AND IMPACT

Internal Audit and IT Audit

Series Editor: Dan Swanson, Dan Swanson and Associates, Ltd., Winnipeg, Manitoba, Canada

The Internal Audit and IT Audit series publishes leading-edge books on critical subjects facing audit executives as well as internal and IT audit practitioners. Key topics include Audit Leadership, Cybersecurity, Strategic Risk Management, Auditing Various IT Activities and Processes, Audit Management, and Operational Auditing.

Say What!?
Communicate with
Tact and Impact

What to Say to Get Results at Any Point in an Audit

Ann M. Butera, CRP

CRC Press
Taylor & Francis Group
Boca Raton London New York

CRC Press is an imprint of the
Taylor & Francis Group, an **informa** business

First edition published 2022
by CRC Press
6000 Broken Sound Parkway NW, Suite 300, Boca Raton, FL 33487-2742

and by CRC Press
2 Park Square, Milton Park, Abingdon, Oxon, OX14 4RN

© 2022 Taylor & Francis Group, LLC

CRC Press is an imprint of Taylor & Francis Group, LLC

ISBN: 978-0-367-55553-5 (hbk)
ISBN: 978-1-032-05773-6 (pbk)
ISBN: 978-1-003-09397-8 (ebk)

DOI: 10.1201/9781003093978

Typeset in Caslon
by SPi Technologies India Pvt Ltd (Straive)

Contents

Preface

It is my pleasure to introduce this book and its content. Based on my 40-year career as an external auditor, internal auditor, and then as the Managing Director of the Internal Audit Division at MIS Training Institute (MISTI), I know how important it is to be able to say the right thing at the right time.

When I was Managing Director at MISTI, my responsibilities included speaking at conferences and developing new seminars and symposia. I was also responsible for content and speaker selection. Consequently, I was always on the lookout for talent whenever I attended IIA, ISACA, and other industry events.

I recall attending an IIA International conference and coincidentally, Ann Butera was one of the speakers. Several of the Audit leaders I knew suggested I listen to her. So I did. The one time was all I needed. Her presentation style was lively and engaging, but more importantly, her ideas were spot on and delivered in a no-nonsense yet humorous way. Aside from thoroughly enjoying her presentation I realized how similar our philosophies were. Our working relationship was based on mutual respect and a commitment to helping our clients get the most from their training experiences. We both have the necessary business acumen (me as an auditor and audit manager, Ann as a consultant), but I liked to say that I was the "practitioner, and Ann has the ability to train people to develop the right behaviors."

So, I invited Ann to speak at one of the MISTI events. And that was just the beginning, since she became a regular conference speaker for the organization. Since then, I have had the pleasure of knowing and working with her for over 25 years.

In 2004, MISTI wanted to develop a five-day program for new audit leaders, which we titled "Audit Leadership." This program was a departure from the normal conference fare of 90-minute sessions arranged in tracks. Its goal was to change behavior and help new audit leaders create value for their organizations and build strong and productive teams. Our strategy was to leverage my prior hands-on audit management experience and include the perspective and objectivity of someone else who was already recognized as a "behavior-changer" in the profession.

I immediately thought of Ann. She was the natural choice because she possessed the curiosity, professional skepticism, and most of all, fascination with procedural efficiency and reliability, and professional development. Audit Leadership was a huge success. Her style and mine meshed perfectly. We covered strategic, tactical, and interpersonal subjects like how to get and keep your seat at the C-Suite table, how to enhance Board and Audit Committee relationships and reporting, and how to deliver bad news.

This program was such a success that Ann and I developed a three-day program for chief audit executives, where we addressed issues like developing the department's vision and how to be the trusted advisor and go-to business partner.

So, this book is timely and on target with its emphasis on communicating with impact and tact, influencing others, overcoming pushback, and resolving conflict should it happen. This is a practical handbook for all internal audit departments. These topics are not just applicable to internal auditors, they are important to risk managers, forensics teams, SOX and COSO testers, and all those who are trying to enhance the control environment.

Having worked so closely with Ann, I see the value and practicality of her approach, which aligns so closely with mine. We both recognize that effective communication is an integral part of getting your findings addressed. Her techniques and mental models are fact-based and intuitive, time-tested by thousands of professionals. I hope you benefit from them as others have.

Joel Kramer

1

PURPOSE

Great minds have purposes, others have wishes.

Washington Irving
American short story writer

1.1 Why a Book on Communication?

We learned to talk and communicate as children, so it's not an unfamiliar behavior. And, as adults we all have had to communicate, providing status reports, sharing ideas, persuading, delivering bad news about topics that are generally strategic, technical, or business related. While communicating may be a commonplace occurrence, how many times do we consciously focus on the quality and effectiveness of the communication?

I have been fascinated by relationships and communication for as long as I can remember. Why we like some people and don't like others. Why we find it easy and fun to work with some people and others not so much.

This book has been on my to-do list for a while. Initially, I started it in 1995. It was the first and only time I cancelled a project because I was overwhelmed by the scope and depth of the topic. More importantly, I realize now with the benefit of 20-20 hindsight that I didn't have the answers. Now, 25 years later, thousands of contracts, training sessions, and conversations later, I have many ideas and time-tested approaches to share.

The purpose of *Say What!? Communicate with Tact and Impact: What to Say to Get Results at Any Point in an Audit* is to provide you with the models and tactics needed to (1) develop and build relationships with your constituents and clients, (2) facilitate productive conversations and discussions before and during meetings, (3) handle impromptu questions with confidence and executive presence, and (4) make positive first impressions. This book contains tips for getting the results you want in your business relationships. That said, you could also use many of these techniques in your personal life.

"Ann, how would you handle this situation" is probably the most frequently asked question during my training sessions because technical expertise isn't enough. Facts aren't enough. Being right isn't enough. Knowing what to say and how to say matters. Being able to find the right word to express what you want to say matters. And, finding the right word is definitely challenging if one works in a multi-cultural environment. During my undergraduate days, I was a French major with a business minor, so I know how hard it is to develop a comprehensive vocabulary in one language, let alone in two or more!

While each person's situation is different, there are some general dos and don'ts for interacting and communicating with others. And, if you are in a technical role and need to collaborate with people who are not technical – or at least not technical in the same way you are – communicating can be tricky. Add country-cultural, generational, and gender differences to the mix and it's amazing that both parties in a conversation understand each other.

Have you ever stopped to think about how much time you spend communicating either in person, by phone, or virtually? It's the primary way we obtain information and exchange ideas. During the course of a day, we deliver thousands of messages – verbally and non-verbally – to our bosses, our clients, our colleagues – not to mention our friends and family. All of our messages shape perceptions of and reactions to us and they shape our outcomes.

The more we interact with the same people, the more these people's perceptions and reactions to us become solidified…and the next thing we know, we have developed a reputation – which may or may not be the one we want or feel we should have.

If people's perceptions and reactions to us are favorable, then our reputation is favorable as well. And, as this positive reputation spreads as a result of networking and time, people will want to work with us. Or, at least, when they find out that they are being audited or reviewed they won't dread it as much. Conversely, if we have developed a less-than-stellar reputation for being a clear communicator, interacting with colleagues and constituents can become more complicated. People may try to postpone the audit or project, or limit its scope as a way to avoid working with us. Constituents may come up with excuses for delayed responses to our requests and questions.

As auditors, risk managers, and assurance professionals, what we say and how we say is critical to the success of our projects. We rely on our communication skills from the moment we begin to plan our engagement and collect the information we need to set the work's scope and objectives. How we phrase our emails and interview questions sets the stage for our relationship with those we audit and work with. Our ability to create rapport with others, make them feel comfortable and at ease, and communicate with impact and tact sets the tone for the audit and forms the foundation of our business relationships.

And, depending on the outcome of your project, you may have to deliver bad news without engendering bad feelings and while creating the greatest amount of buy-in to a corrective action plan and series of next steps. Once again, the ability to communicate with empathy and accuracy is integral to our ability to achieve useful results and create value.

This book is for you if you are in a technical field and you need to communicate and persuade people who are not technical and who may have educations, backgrounds, and experiences that are very different than yours. *Say What!? Communicate with Tact and Impact* focuses on the following core competencies:

- Presenting to the Board, senior management, process owners, control owners, and colleagues.
- Facilitating opening or kick off meetings, planning sessions, status meetings, and closing (or exit) conferences.
- Influencing business managers to agree to address control gaps, design flaws, and execution errors.
- Positioning messages for positive impact.
- Anticipating and addressing audience needs.
- Preventing and handling difficult situations.
- Delivering bad news.
- Responding to pushback and objections.
- Managing disagreements to prevent conflict.

It covers ways to establish your executive presence and increase your ability to be the trusted advisor. And, it covers when you need to stop – when you've tried enough and it's time to move on.

Now that you know what the book is about, let me tell you what it's not. It's not a script. It's not a one-size-fits-all approach to interacting with people in the organization. Given the diversity of personalities and range of motivations, it is impossible to prescribe exact wording. This book is a source of strategies and tactics. It provides practical, time-tested approaches, models, and guidance that you can adapt to suit the situation, the other person's style, and your goals.

If you are new to the profession, view this book as primer, providing communication guidance and tactics for the typical situations you would encounter during planning, testing, and reporting. Focus on the techniques for instilling trust, projecting executive presence, and running effective meetings.

If you are an experienced auditor, risk management, information security, or assurance professional, focus on the techniques for overcoming objections and handling audit negotiations, which are more specialized than the typical scenarios one would encounter when buying a car or selling a house.

Whether you are new or experienced in auditing, risk management, information security, or general assurance work, the advice and techniques in this book are intended to make you a better communicator during in-person, telephone, and video conferences at every stage of your audit, project, or review. Culled from over 30 years' experience working with thousands of professionals in an array of industries, these approaches are time-tested and will enable you to deliver the right message to get results at any point in your audit or project.

I send special thanks to those who agreed to review my ideas and share their reactions and thoughts – all of which have made my message clearer and this book better:

Dan Swanson
Mariel Cruz
Audley Bell
Martha Jane Gagnon
Trent Russell
Lori Klebous

Rocio Arvizo-Huerta
Felix Vargas
Christine Carney
Mary A. Lochner
Matt Cesaro
Dan Samson
Michelle Piranio
Marion Manchester

I look forward to hearing your comments and questions as you put the practical techniques into action and communicate with tact and impact.

2

How to Get the Most from This Book

Change might not be fast and it isn't always easy. But with time and effort, almost any habit can be reshaped.

Charles Duhigg

The Power of Habit: Why We Do What We Do in Life and Business

I started this chapter by quoting Charles Duhigg because acquiring the skills discussed in this book are really a matter of developing the right habits.

I never realized the importance of habits until I started playing tennis. Although I took tennis lessons as a teenager, I didn't play in earnest until I was an adult. By that time, I had to apply myself to be able to compete with people who had played high school and college tennis. The tennis lessons I had as an adult enabled me to realize the benefit of having a plan, consistent performance, and productive habits.

I remember one of my tennis instructors asking me if I believed that practice makes one perfect. "Of course," was my reply, because this was a value that had been drummed into me as a little kid. "Well, it's not true," he said. "Practice doesn't make perfect, only perfect practice makes perfect." Wow! Until then, I hadn't really thought about it, but he was right. If I spent time using the wrong techniques or choosing the wrong shot or targeting the wrong direction, I was simply reinforcing these bad behaviors and committing them to muscle memory. Not a good use of time or energy.

My preoccupation with practicing the right behaviors and developing productive habits has continued and moved from the tennis court to my work as a trainer and an organizational development (OD) consultant. I know that what matters is what you *do* (i.e., your behavior and actions), not just what you *know*.

As OD specialists, my team and I work with managers to define what good performance looks like. That is, what are the observable, measurable attributes that are present when work performance is effective and people are meeting their goals. We then study the under-performers to understand and identify their actions. Essentially, we're looking for observable, measurable behavioral patterns. We analyze these patterns and deconstruct them into their component parts and competencies so we can use this information to define what good looks like for a particular organization or situation. Then, we use this information to develop recruitment strategies so that our clients can hire effective performers. We document the approaches that the good performers use to define sound, consistent, repeatable workflows and processes. And, we develop training programs to teach others the skills, approaches, competencies, and habitual behaviors they need to produce effective and consistent results.

As you read and plan how you will use the strategies and techniques I describe, keep one thing in mind: your preferred interpersonal and communication style affects how you perceive and interact with others and how they perceive and interact with you. Your behavioral style affects how you communicate and whether you use short, simple, direct sentences or whether you express your messages in highly descriptive terms. Your style affects the degree to which you are goal-oriented or people-oriented. Your style acts like a filter to all of your communication – whether you are speaking or writing.

To identify and understand different communication styles, I have used a simple assessment that enables individuals to categorize their own behavioral preferences. During my career, I have assessed and profiled thousands of audit, risk, ERM, and compliance professionals ranging from stall auditors to chief audit executives and chief risk officers. My conclusions concerning each of the behavioral styles are summarized below. If you are not sure of your preferred communication style or someone else's, consider which of the following best describes you and the individuals with whom you work.

STYLE	BEHAVIORAL PROFILE	TYPICAL % OF RESPONSES
Analytical	Is systematic and well-organized, and craves data. Sets very high standards (i.e., perfectionism) and is willing to do the time-consuming work needed to meet these standards and is very hard on self and others. Wants things to be right. Therefore, can agonize over decisions. When facing risks, is prudent and approaches situations logically. Is sparing with compliments and expressions of appreciation and shows little emotion. Uses low-key body language. Like to be alone or with just a few people. Under stress, experiences analysis paralysis.	40%
Vocalizer	Is very talkative and can use talking to think through ideas. Is able to convey complex concepts in simple terms. Uses engaging language and persuasive wording. Is very warm, friendly, social, and responsive to people. Tends to tell stories and slips from one topic to another. When facing risks tends to focus on the "big picture" (i.e., how the risk would affect the organization as a whole), not the function in which the vulnerability exists. Tends to be a poor listener and loses interest when discussions become very detailed or routine. Uses emphatic and forceful body language. Under stress becomes impatient and speaks quickly and loudly.	5%
Bottom-liner	Is very task-oriented. Derives great satisfaction in completing assignments. Is easily frustrated when unable to complete tasks. Likes to do things in his or her own way and avoid restraints. Is energetic and fast-paced. Offers opinions easily and is very candid and direct in communication. Tends to be a poor listener. Uses forceful body language like the Vocalizer. Under stress becomes overly directive and less collaborative.	25%
People Pleaser	Is people-oriented and a team player. Is very open to the opinions of others. Typically performs best in stable, clearly structured situations. Is comfortable doing routine procedures and following processes established by others. Takes a cautious approach to decision-making and may be indecisive especially when the decision requires doing something new or different from what has been done before. Prefers face-to-face or phone conversations instead of emails. Values harmonious working relationships and avoids conflicts. Under stress becomes passive and goes along with the group decision to avoid disagreement.	30%

Today's actions, if repeated, become tomorrow's habits. So, you need to be aware of what you are doing that enables you to achieve the results you want. You also need to know what doesn't work and hinders your ability to achieve your desired results. Once you know what works and what doesn't – and when it works and when it doesn't – you are in a powerful position to control how you communicate and work with anyone under any circumstances.

Although you need to adapt your behavior to optimize buy-in and agreement from others, you simultaneously need to remain true to the message you want to send as well as to your values, the facts, and your goal (i.e., improving the organization's risk management culture and practices). This means that you need to speak up about the facts and the other person's reactions to them as well as the implications of the other person's risk appetite and tolerance. And most importantly, you need to be able to communicate these messages in a way that does not seem condescending, self-serving, or self-interested.

This book's content is culled from over 30 years of experience consulting with hundreds of organizations and teaching thousands of professionals. It contains practical techniques, advice, and tips that you can put to use immediately. It provides time-tested ideas that will save you time, reduce your stress, and produce reliable, quality results.

This book addresses proven techniques grounded in solid psychological and sociological theory applied to typical business situations encountered by risk management, information security, compliance, internal auditors, and business professionals in all industries.

Like *Five Tiers of Audit Competency*, the approaches described in this book focus on the behaviors you need at any point to manage the people relationships as well as the work. These approaches and models will enable you to develop the best habits when communicating with others at any point during an audit or review.

Although I've organized the skills in the order in which you would need to use them if you were starting a project or audit, I began with two abilities you need all the time: *Projecting Executive Presence* (Chapter 3) and *How to Be the Trusted Advisor* (Chapter 4).

Your executive presence affects how others perceive and react to you – sometimes before you can say anything. *How to Be the Trusted Advisor* describes the behaviors that cause others to view you as a credible and reliable professional – someone they can approach to discuss issues they may have on their minds.

These two behaviors form a foundation for the remaining skills and techniques that the book covers:

- Influencing Others for Results
- Facilitating Meetings and Discussions
- Speaking with Tact, Confidence, and Impact
- Delivering Bad News without Causing Bad Feelings
- Overcoming Objections and Resistance
- Managing and Resolving Conflict
- Specialized Negotiations Skills
- When to Let Go and Move On

Although you certainly could read this book from cover to cover, you don't have to. You can just read about the techniques and situations that interest you or are important to you. Or, just read what you need to address the situations you face. Each chapter stands on its own.

At each chapter's end, I have included a section entitled *For Skill Practice* that describes activities to help you apply the techniques, reinforce your positive behavioral change, and continue to develop your skills. If you are part of a team, you might want to do the activities as a group or use them to spark discussions about professional development during staff meetings.

If you are serious about creating useful habits and making a lasting change in your life, complete the *Takeaway Game Plan* at the end of each chapter. It will help you target the specific actions you need to take to create positive change as well as ways to measure your progress over time.

As the Chinese philosopher Lao Tzu said, "The journey of a thousand miles must begin with one step." What step will you take to be your best self? I look forward to hearing about your progress.

3

PROJECTING EXECUTIVE PRESENCE

No man or woman attains a top job, lands an extraordinary deal, or develops a significant following without this heady combination of confidence, poise, and authenticity – that convinces the rest of us we are in the presence of someone who is the real deal.

Sylvia Ann Hewlett
Economist and Author of *Executive Presence: The Missing Link between Merit and Success*

Have you ever tried to define "executive presence" and found yourself struggling for words? If so, you are not alone. Trying to describe these attributes can leave you feeling frustrated. Yet, you definitely recognize executive presence when you see someone that has it. And, just as easily you can spot the person that just does not have it.

Yet, it isn't enough to simply say "I know executive presence when I see it in someone." While "I know it when I see it" worked in 1964 for United States Supreme Court Justice Potter Stewart to describe this threshold test for obscenity in the case *Jacobellis v Ohio*, this approach won't enable you to recruit the appropriate candidate to fill an opening in your team (and it might get you in trouble with your Human Resources generalist). It will not enable you to provide useful performance feedback to your direct reports (and may even frustrate them, cause them to question your judgment, and get you another meeting with your Human Resources generalist). And, it won't help you develop and grow as a professional.

So, let's use the following behavioral approach to define what it means to have executive presence. Think about a person who, in your opinion, demonstrates executive presence. This individual may be someone you know or report to at work, or it may be someone you

DOI: 10.1201/9781003093978-3

13

don't know personally but have seen or heard speak at a conference. In the space below, describe the things this person does that signal executive presence. It may be easier for you to put your audit critical thinking hat on and identify the things this person does or says that provides evidence that he or she has executive presence.

Indicators or Evidence That Someone Has Executive Presence

Now, mentally step back and compare what you have written to the following three components of executive presence:

External Packaging
Mental Acuity
Personal Values

The combination of these three components creates a condition that enables an individual to project calmness, confidence, integrity, and approachability. Let's consider each component more closely, beginning with the External Packaging.

3.1 External Packaging

External Packaging is probably the one most people associate with executive presence because it is literally the most obvious. It is the physical image that people see or the sound that they hear when a person speaks. External Packaging encompasses:

- Work-appropriate attire and accessories. "Work-appropriate" is definitely a situationally dependent concept affected by a number of factors that is not limited to industry, job role, work medium (e.g., remote versus live), and organizational policy. Essentially, work-appropriate attire is a relative concept. Decisions determining whether one's attire is work appropriate involve considering what one person is wearing compared to what other people in the same environment are wearing. In more traditional organizations, work-appropriate attire may consist of suits. In more informal cultures, work-appropriate attire may consist of jeans and t-shirts (as long as the t-shirts are slogan-and message-free).

What is considered work-appropriate in your organization?

- Posture. How one positions one's body when seated or standing conveys a message to others. For example, in the US, leaning forward in one's chair when speaking with others during a meeting projects confidence and energy (and aggression, if overdone). Leaning backward or sinking into one's chair (assuming it is comfortable enough to do this) indicates disinterest or distancing from the topic under discussion.

What impression does your body language convey during a group-live or virtual meeting? Is your body language giving others the impression you want them to have?

- Behavior. Others' perceptions concerning your executive presence is affected by whether one actively or passively engages with others during one-on-one conversations or group meetings. Active engagement with others is characterized by initiating conversations and exchanges with others without prompting and asking questions to satisfy a native curiosity. Someone who is actively engaged contributes (relevantly) to discussions by asking questions or providing information without being asked to do so. If one is passively engaged, one responds or contributes when asked to do so. One's behavior also provides signposts concerning personal and work values. For example, imagine that a person chronically arrives late to meetings. While there may be reasons for this individual's tardiness, others who witness this form opinions.

How would others describe your behavior during virtual and in-person meetings? Would they view you as typically engaged? Distant? Passive?

- Facial expressions. The ability to be aware of and manage one's facial expressions (i.e., remain calm under pressure) is an indicator of executive presence. For example, imagine that someone is telling you some really, really bad news. Are you aware of how your facial expression is changing as you hear and process this message? During virtual meetings, your camera's angle and the lighting in front of your monitor can enhance or detract from your image. If your camera is angled up and facing the ceiling, you will look like you are hunched down. If the camera is facing a brightly lit window behind you, no one will be able to see your face because of the back lighting.

  If you have executive presence, you are able to maintain a neutral expression although inwardly you may be reeling from the information you received. Other times it is important to convey excitement and happiness. Imagine that your team has just exceeded a performance goal or has accomplished a special project that was strategically important. Under these circumstances, those who have executive presence are able to convey via facial expression unmistakable excitement and enthusiasm.

How does your facial expression change when you are under stress? Frustrated? Happy? Confused? What impressions are you giving others?

- Voice. This factor has a couple of dimensions that affect perception of executive presence: loudness, lilt, and speed. People who have executive presence project their voice audibly so that others do not struggle to hear the message. People who have executive presence make statements (i.e., their voices do not rise at the end of a sentence as though they were asking a question). People who have executive presence speak at a steady rate – not too slow as to seem like they are speaking to a remedial group, nor too fast as to seem like they are trying to hoodwink the listeners.

  Following are things that you can do to use your voice to increase your executive presence:

  - Minimize audible pauses and speech fillers. Audible pauses are the sounds that come out of your mouth while you are waiting for your think time and speech to get into alignment. Essentially, you have run out of things to say but sounds like "um" or fillers (e.g., like, you know, obviously) keep coming out of your mouth. (Refer to Chapter 7 for ways to reduce audible pauses.)
  - Ensure that body language and rate of speech conform to your message. You wouldn't use the same tone to convey good news as you would bad news. (Refer to Chapter 8 for ways to deliver bad news to others.)
  - Use brief, true war stories and analogies to accentuate key points in your verbal communications. A war story is a short, true anecdote that exemplifies the point you want to make.
  - Speak in shorter, clearer sentences because they are easy for others to understand.

- Use more vibrant and distinctive language to convey your ideas. Use similes and metaphors to create memorable comparisons and mental imagery.

What is your typical speech quality? If you are not sure, how often do people ask you to repeat what you said (an indicator that your speech was too fast, too soft, or too slurred)? You might want to ask a trusted colleague to listen to you and provide helpful feedback.

- Etiquette. According to the Oxford Dictionary, the definition of etiquette is the customary code of polite behavior in society or among members of a particular profession or group.

People may hear your words, but they feel your body language.

John C. Maxell

an American author, speaker, and pastor

Different social situations have certain rules – ones that may or may not be published. People who have executive presence demonstrate behavior that complies with these rules. Essentially, they are aware of and comply with the social mores and norms. Let me give you an example.

Imagine that you are at a restaurant, seated at a table of six. Everyone has ordered and is enjoying appetizers and drinks while awaiting the entrees. The waiter begins to deliver the dinners – one at a time to everyone. When the waiter sets your dinner plate in front of you, what do you do?

1. Option 1: You start eating immediately because you don't want the food to get cold (and you are starving because this dinner is later than you would normally eat).

2. Option 2: You wait to make sure that everyone has received a meal before tasting yours.

Option 2 is the correct answer if you want to display etiquette according to Emily Post.[1] The polite behavior is to wait until everyone receives a meal or until the person who has not been served says it's okay to proceed.

Now, you may have read this and say to yourself, "Finally, someone who understands etiquette! It has upset me to have been at these dinners where everyone starts eating the minute food is placed in front of him or her as though each person was starving and hasn't seen food in a decade."

On the other hand, you may have read this and say to yourself, "Are you kidding? Why wait until everyone is served? My meal is here and hot. If I wait it will start to congeal."

These two reactions are polar. Why? The difference is the understanding of socially acceptable behavior or etiquette, which is affected by culture.

Etiquette for Virtual Meetings

Etiquette for virtual meetings is relatively new and includes:

- Logging on a few minutes early to make sure you don't have connection issues so that meetings can begin on time.
- Turning your camera on if others' cameras are on. And, if you can't, letting the others (at a minimum the meeting host) know why (e.g., you are experiencing bandwidth issues or your camera is not working).
- Using photos to create a virtual background when working in communal at-home areas.
- Keeping your mike on mute unless you are speaking so that distracting background noises are eliminated.
- Not eating while on camera….who really needs to have a close-up view of another person chewing?
- Sliding slightly out of frame to sip (not gulp) a beverage like water or tea.

What is the etiquette in your organization?

- Email. Consider how often people form their first impression of you based on your email because they have not or may not meet you in person or virtually. The content, layout, and tone of your email and other online communications send a distinct message about your executive presence.

Following are some ways to make sure that your emails complement – not undermine – your executive presence:

- If you are using a template, make sure its content is completely applicable and its tone is appropriate for the level and role of the person to whom you are sending it. Is the tone too formal? Too informal? Is all the content relevant? If you answer no to any of these questions, adjust the content before pressing send.
- Start by writing a draft unless your message is a simple, one line message. Read it out loud (to identify missing words, run-ons, and messy messages).
- If the message concerns a tough topic or difficult matter, don't fill in the recipient's email address – you don't want to accidentally press send before you have had a chance to reflect on your message. Save the email in drafts to send later in the day. This habit gives you the option of rechecking or editing your work before you hit send.
- Make sure your call-to-action is easy to spot. In fact, you might want to put it in the subject line, so it grabs the reader's attention and summarizes your message. Be sure to keep the title catchy and short.
- Keep the entire message short and to the point. Use attachments for longer documents, especially since many receive and read their emails on their phone. If you can't avoid writing a long email, be sure to use subheadings for the benefit of those who are reading quickly or need to see the key points quickly.
- Do not send an email when you are angry. In fact, it's probably best to cool down before doing anything when you are angry. Once you calm down, you may realize that picking up the phone or getting on a video call to talk to the other person makes more sense than firing back a written reply that is devoid of intonation and nuance. And, of course, do not write anything in an email that you wouldn't want posted or shared with others.

- Double check all of the recipients' email addresses when writing to several people at once before pressing send. You want all recipients to receive the message at the same time and you don't want to discover that you need to resend to someone. At the same time, consider whether everyone on your list needs to receive the message you're sending. There's an inverse relationship between the number of people on a distribution list and the number of people who actually read the email. This means the more people on the distribution less, the fewer who read it. Why? Most people are inundated with emails. If they see one with a long distribution list, they think: Since so many are getting this message, one of them will do something with it. Curate your distribution list with care. As a general rule, copy those mentioned in the email and only those who need to act on the message.
- If you are sending an attachment, make sure the file is actually attached before pressing send. I have found it helpful to attach the file immediately when I start the email message.
- Use the spellchecker, and then proof the message. Most email spellcheckers can check for spelling errors, but will not pick up grammatical or word misuses, for example, *there* versus *their* versus *they're*.
- Don't blindly copy because you never know who will forward it.

If you will deliver your message virtually, you will need to think about your virtual image and what it is telling others about you.

- Turn on your camera and study the items that comprise the background. Do the things in the background seem cluttered or create a distraction? If so, clear the background or move the laptop to a different space.
- If you plan to use a virtual background, consider something neutral or maybe a photo of the office. Ocean and mountain views – particularly when they include motion, are distracting for the viewers.

- Consider the message your background sends to others about you. For example, you may want your background to capture your degrees, specific artwork, or sports trophies so that you can use them as an icebreaker when starting a meeting.
- Pay attention to the locations of window and natural light that are behind you because this backlighting will make it difficult for others to see your face. Eliminate this problem by drawing blinds or shades tightly.
- Make it easy for the other people in your virtual meeting to see your expressions by a) setting up your laptop in front of a window, so that the natural light provides the key lighting or b) setting up your key lighting directly behind your laptop's camera. Ideally, this lighting should be somewhat downward to completely illuminate your face.
- Make sure that you have sufficient surface area around your computer so that you can access your notes while you communicate your message.
- Prior to delivering your message, be sure to open all the files you will need during your presentation so you can easily access and share them.

3.2 Mental Acuity

Now, let's consider the second component of executive presence, Mental Acuity. Acuity refers to quickness, keenness, or sharpness and is assessed by others based on an individual's experience, insight, and intelligence. Let's look at each of these attributes in detail.

- Experience. This is the practical contact with others, involvement in activities, and observation of facts or events that occurs multiple times a day, each day of your life. Everything you do in life contributes to your experience, and over time, this experience becomes your personal data store. Unconsciously, you compare new situations that are similar to familiar ones to form opinions and make decisions.

  The level and nature of experience varies by person. For example, some people may have lived in several different countries or worked for a number of organizations or held a variety of different jobs. People with executive presence are aware that everyone's experience is different and are mindful of this when they communicate and interact with others. They do not assume that everyone shares a common experience and has the same reaction to messages and situations.

What type of experience do you have? How consistent or varied is it?

- Insight. This is the ability to gain a deep and accurate understanding of a situation, something, or someone. When you have an insight, you have a feeling or emotion or thought that helps you to know something essential about a person or thing. When you gain insight, you are using your intuition, or sixth sense. Of course, the word intuition and references to a sixth sense can sound squishy and unreliable….hardly the behaviors one would expect to see in an auditor or risk professional. However, think of intuition as the amalgamation of all of the learning experiences you have had during your life. It would be impossible to recall each experience specifically; however, when you encounter a new person or situation, you are actually tapping into this combined store of experiences, enabling you to respond and have insight. You may have wondered why some people are insightful and others not so much. Different people have different levels of experience because each person's combined experiences is different. Also, some people have had more experience and more diversified experience than others. And finally, some people do not learn from their experiences and live their lives as though they were in the movie Groundhog Day.[2]

How insightful are you? Have your team members or constituents commented on your ability to notice things that others haven't?

- Intelligence. This is the ability to acquire and apply general knowledge and skills, and use them to reason and draw conclusions. Some people are naturally more adept at learning new things and gaining new capabilities than others. People with executive presence are able to absorb and process new information without letting the inherent pressure when learning new things stress them out. They remain calm under pressure.

How do you react when you have to learn new things?

- Technical knowledge. Unlike general knowledge, these are the abilities and information needed to perform specialized tasks like auditing, inherent risk assessment, control evaluation, data analysis, and testing. Having executive presence does not mean that you know everything. You need to be able recognize the gaps in the resources you have and rely on others for help.

What type of technical knowledge do you have? What steps do you take when you have to build technical knowledge in a new subject or area?

3.3 Personal Values

The last component, personal values, like Mental Acuity, is assessed by others based on an individual's actions, statements, and decisions. This component is comprised of personal norms and philosophy (the usual, typical, or standard rules you follow to make decisions, judge others' behavior, and interact with others), integrity, honesty, sincerity, initiative, optimism, and relationship building. While these traits are intrinsically intangible, they are frequently used by others when considering whether a person has executive presence.

The degree to which you behave authentically, with consistent integrity and honesty, and are able to establish and build relationships enables others to see you as a person with executive presence. Being authentic means being true to yourself and your uniqueness. You can possess executive presence and still express your individuality and personal values; you do not have to imitate another person.

How would another person describe your personal values?

Executive Presence is an interesting concept because the determination as to whether you have it is made by other people, not you. You might think that you have all of the attributes described in this chapter and consequently demonstrate executive presence. But what you think doesn't count. It's what other people think that matters. How effectively you demonstrate each of these factors contributes directly to another person's judgment as to whether you have executive presence.

IMAGE REALLY DOES MATTER

After I left banking and before I started The Whole Person Project, Inc., I spent about 9 months in recruiting (AKA headhunting) and my target market was internal audit and accounting professionals. Ishkibiddle (not his real name) was one of the candidates that I had identified as a good fit for an open audit manager position in a 30-person department. He met all of the requirements and I thought he would be a good cultural fit as well.

I set up the interview with the hiring authority, who was the Chief Audit Executive, and met with Ishkibiddle one more time to make sure he was prepared. The meeting was the next morning at 10 am and I was already wondering how quickly Ishkibiddle could start the new position.

The next day, I was expecting to hear from Ishkibiddle as soon as the interview ended because I preferred to hear from the candidates before speaking with the hiring authority. When it was almost 1 pm and I still hadn't heard from Ishkibiddle, I began to get concerned and tried to reach him at home. No answer. I waited 30 minutes and tried again without any result.

Finally, late in the day, I decided to call the hiring authority and get his feedback. The Chief Audit Executive minced no words in telling me that he was completely unimpressed and almost annoyed by Ishkibiddle during the interview to the point that the CAE was questioning my ability to screen and select suitable candidates. Oh boy, my stomach twisted with stress and I was so stupefied that I could barely find my voice to ask what had happened. "Well, let's start with the fact that this guy had the clammiest handshake ever (this interview occurred well before COVID-19 pandemic when people were still meeting in public and shaking hands) and during the interview, he was sweating and could barely stay focused to answer my questions. He made very little eye contact and generally seemed like he wanted to by anywhere by my office."

Wow! This description did not sound like the Ishkibiddle I knew. Hours later that day I was finally able to reach Ishkibiddle at home. Trying to control my confusion and frustration – not to mention my embarrassment because my relationship with the hiring authority took a hit from this experience – I asked Ishkibiddle what happened. He apologized for not calling earlier but the whole day he had been feeling as though he had the flu. In fact, he thought about canceling the interview that morning but decided to go anyway even though his hands felt sweaty. When I asked Ishkibiddle whether he told the CAE how he was feeling, Ishkibiddle said he didn't think it was necessary to do that.

Ishkibiddle's poor judgment cost him the job. The CAE never knew Ishkibiddle was not feeling well but the CAE knew Ishkibiddle lacked the executive presence to fill the position.

For Skill Practice

If you are wondering how to increase your executive presence, you can take the following actions:

- Dress in attire that is appropriate for your company and industry. If you are in the early stages of your career, pay attention to what the executives and senior managers are wearing.
- Make steady, sincere, and comfortable eye contact with everyone you meet.
- Use smooth and natural hand gestures to make your points. Avoid forceful finger pointing.
- Make sure your posture is straight, not slumped, to project confidence.
- Smile so you project an open and friendly expression.
- Speak loudly enough so that everyone can hear you and speak slowly enough so that your words are enunciated (not slurred together) and others can understand what you are saying.
- Be gracious and punctual, demonstrating office etiquette and good team member behavior.
- Demonstrate a working knowledge of the subject under discussion.
- Display your technical understanding and proficiency.
- Leverage your resources and ask for help when you need it – having executive presence means knowing what you know and what you don't.
- Show a positive outlook concerning your work and projects.
- Do as you say (i.e., walk the talk) to show integrity, sincerity, and consistency.
- Project competency through increased organization and steady eye contact.

- Minimize audible pauses and speech fillers.
- Ensure that body language and rate of speech conforms with your message.
- Pay more attention to details in your appearance and your work products.
- Use brief, true war stories and analogies to accentuate key points in your verbal communications.
- Speak in shorter, clearer sentences.
- Use more vibrant and distinctive language to convey your ideas.

Chapter Summary

- The three components of executive presence are: external packaging, mental acuity, and personal values.
- Having these three components creates a condition that enables you to project calmness, confidence, integrity, and approachability.
- If you have executive presence, you are able to maintain a neutral expression although inwardly you may be reeling from the information you received.

Notes

1 **Emily Post,** American authority on social behavior who crafted her advice by applying good sense and thoughtfulness to basic human interactions.
2 Groundhog Day is a comedy movie directed by Harold Ramis and written by Ramis and Danny Rubin. It stars Bill Murray as Phil Connors, a TV weatherman who, during an assignment covering the annual Groundhog Day event, is caught in a time loop, repeatedly reliving the same day.

My Takeaway Game Plan

My Goal is:

Behaviors I will *start* to achieve my goal...

Behaviors I will *continue* to achieve my goal...

Behaviors I will *stop* to achieve my goal...

Leading and Lagging Indicators – How I'll Measure My Results

4

HOW TO BE THE TRUSTED ADVISOR

Trust is like blood pressure. It's silent, vital to good health, and if abused it can be deadly.

Frank Sonneberg
Author of Follow Your Conscience

What behaviors and traits come to mind when you think of someone who is a trusted advisor? Perhaps this question is easier to answer if you think about the person or people (if you are extra lucky to have more than one) in your life who you view as your trusted advisor.

When I ask this question to participants in my training sessions, they describe trusted advisors as people who are:

- Honest and will tell me when I am part of the problem.
- Dependable – this person is there when needed.
- Knowledgeable about the issue or situation I need to discuss.
- Experienced (either in a specific area or in general life).
- Truthful – even when they have to tell me bad news.
- Able to keep confidences.
- Interested in my success.
- Supportive and let me know they have my back.
- Easy to talk to – even when the subject is a difficult one.
- Helpful and want the best for me (i.e., want me to succeed).

I deliberately ask people to describe the behaviors or characteristics (as opposed to attitudes or mental outlooks) of those they view as trusted advisors because we can emulate and imitate behaviors. Behaviors are observable and measurable; mental outlooks and attitudes are not. For example, if you are fortunate enough to have a trusted advisor, consider why this person has decided to fill this role and be your trusted advisor. Assuming this person is not one of your parents, do you really know your trusted advisor's motivation? Although you may guess the

DOI: 10.1201/9781003093978-4 **31**

motivation, you really will never be sure unless the person tells you. And, even then, your trusted advisor may not be able to express the exact reasons that caused this special relationship to form. In fact, this person may not view his or her role in your life as one of a trusted advisor. This person may never have considered labeling your relationship this way.

So, instead of focusing on labels and attitudes, concentrate on behaviors: yours and the other person's. Is this person giving you sound advice, drawn from experience that is intended to help you succeed? Are you participating in tough conversations during which this person (your trusted advisor) suggests that you may be part of the problem you are trying to solve? These behaviors are associated with trusted advisor relationships, regardless of whether you have labeled the relationship as such. Focusing on behavior instead of attitude streamlines the situation and makes it easier to receive information and take action.

Consider this situation from a completely different perspective. Some organizations have buddy programs and mentor programs for new hires or those who have been identified as high-potential employees. A component of these programs is to pair employees with experienced team members or senior managers. Simply pairing people together does not mean that any relationship will form – let alone a trusted advisor relationship.

WHAT MOTIVATED JANE

One of the many volunteer positions I have had during my career was Chairman of the Board for a local franchise of a national nonprofit youth organization. At the time, I was around 30 years old and my predecessor was my mother's age.

In this role, I worked very closely with Jane Cammann, an experienced Executive Director who was 30 years my senior. When I describe Jane as experienced, I mean that she was a career executive director, committed to the national franchise's mission and adept at navigating the inherently political environment that required an ability to balance the needs of the national organization, the local franchise, and the objects of our work: the volunteers and the children we served.

I enjoyed the work and approached it with the enthusiasm one has at 30. Jane and I tackled every issue and obstacle that confronted us (including having the site of our office declared a SuperFund site and getting it delisted – but that is a story for another time).

If an issue was particularly thorny, strategic, or difficult, we would spend hours discussing it together and with others to come up with the best solution. While Jane and I didn't always agree – in fact we sometimes argued because we had opposing views on the action we needed to take – we respected each other and worked very well together.

At some point, I don't know exactly when, we started to discuss more than just the issues facing the franchise. I shared issues facing my business and she offered advice, which I gratefully accepted. Somehow, my relationship with Jane morphed into a trusted advisor relationship.

In 1993, Jane retired to Vero Beach, Florida. When my work relationship with Jane ended, our friendship was able to expand since she no longer reported to me and each of us was able to talk about a broader spectrum of topics. Somehow, without any fanfare or discussion, Jane slipped into the role of my trusted advisor. I appreciated her level-headed advice, even when it was that I needed to change or improve something that I was doing.

Jane's behavior epitomizes that of a trusted advisor. She wanted me to succeed but didn't hesitate to tell me when I was contributing or causing the very problem I wanted to resolve. I knew that whatever I told Jane would be treated confidentially. Most importantly, I knew that she wanted the best for me – personally and professionally.

Sadly, Jane passed away in 2012. I still miss her advice. But I am a better person for having had the benefit of her counsel for almost 20 years.

4.1 So....How Do I Become the Trusted Advisor?

"The glue that holds all relationships together including the relationship between the leader and the led – is trust, and trust is based on integrity."

Brian Tracy

Canadian-American motivational public speaker
and self-development author

If you want to be your constituents' trusted advisor, you need to be honest, dependable, and approachable, and you need to demonstrate that your concern about the other person's welfare outweighs your self-interest. You also have to give the relationship some time; it doesn't occur overnight.

You are probably thinking that this sounds too simplistic. Well, as they say, the devil is in the details. How you display each of these behaviors matters. Let me give you a couple of examples by applying these concepts to typical audit and risk management situations.

Let's focus on being honest. What makes you view another person as honest? When I ask this question in my training programs, participants associate the following behaviors with people who are honest:

- The person is truthful.
- The person is believable.
- The answers or information provided is accurate.
- The data provided are complete.
- The information or perspective is balanced (i.e., the pros and the cons are communicated).
- The person doesn't display a bias (or admits that a bias exists when sharing the data).

As you consider the behaviors on this list, they seem natural and even a bit ordinary. Perhaps the most challenging behavior on the list is the one that relates to the ability to provide a balanced perspective.

Let me give you an example. Imagine that you are planning an audit of XYZ and your planning document is intended to cite all the functional areas and then indicate the ones that will be in scope.

You want to focus on the areas of greatest risk to XYZ. As you collect and review information, your mind focuses on high risk and unconsciously filters out information related to low-risk areas, effectively your audit planning and scope documentation focuses on only the high-risk areas. If you haven't acknowledged or cited the low-risk aspects or functions that comprise XYZ, your information is unbalanced.

When you present your planning document to the constituent, who is familiar with the entire XYZ process, the constituent will review the list of functional areas and realize that some are missing (which will trigger the reaction that your document is inaccurate and by association, you are not accurate and consequently not to be believed).

Unless you clearly communicate that your planning documentation only focuses on high-risk areas, the constituent will think that you have excluded areas and do not have a complete understanding of XYZ.

Whenever a person provides information that is subsequently determined to be inaccurate or incomplete, the provider's trustworthiness is impugned and reduced. The inaccuracy may be as simple as a typo or omission (like forgetting to add the word "not" in a sentence completely changes its meaning).

BLAME IT ON THE SYSTEM

I was involved in a series of conversations and emails with a member of a client's Vendor Management team (who I will call Cruella – which is not her real name) to make sure that we would receive payment for our services within 5 days from the date the invoice was received. This was one of the last steps in what had been a several-month long, tedious, detailed process. Cruella told us that all payments could only be issued 45 days after the invoice was received – no exceptions because it was a "system" thing. We thought this was unbelievable, but Cruella was certain and adamant.

During an unrelated conversation with a colleague who works for a friendly competitor, I found out that his company also had to deal with Cruella when his firm was set up for payment. Imagine my reaction when I found out that his firm's invoices are paid within 30 days of receipt! I have not trusted Cruella again and I am extremely skeptical of information that I receive from other employees in that company.

I wonder whether Cruella's behavior was company-sanctioned (i.e., an overt directive or a performance incentive plan that encouraged people to be duplicitous) or simply overzealousness on her part. Months later, when we started a new project with the same company, I stood my ground and secured our desired payment terms.

If you want to be perceived as dependable, you really need to do what you say you will do and honor your commitments. In essence, you need to under promise and over deliver.

Consequently, you should be careful when you say you will do things (e.g., send information, return calls, or schedule meetings). Make sure that you really can meet the deadlines you have communicated to others. Keep in mind that whatever information or reports you intend to send will probably need to be reviewed and these reviews can be delayed.

If something happens and you cannot honor your commitment, you need to explain why before the other person asks (i.e., be proactive). This gives you the opportunity to manage the narrative and explain – in your own words – why you didn't honor your word. (By the way, you can only do this a couple of times before the other person figures out that your word is meaningless.)

4.2 Timeliness

So far, I have focused on honoring commitments you have consciously made to others as a way of demonstrating your dependability, an important component of trustworthiness.

Your general timeliness is another behavioral signal to others of whether you can be trusted. If you are chronically late for meetings, deadlines, and other appointments, this behavior telegraphs unreliability. (Actually, it telegraphs that you can be relied on to be late, which is typically not a desirable quality in a trusted advisor or ordinary team member.)

At a minimum, others will either learn to start without you (which is a precursor to being overlooked or forgotten when assignments are made) or assume that their meetings with you have a lower priority in your life (and who likes to think that he or she isn't a priority?).

At some point, though, everyone is in a situation that prevents them from doing what they said they would do. The cause may be outside your control (e.g., transportation issues like flat tires or train delays) or within it (e.g., oversleeping, illness). When these unfortunate situations occur, the key is how you deal with them (i.e., whether you respond proactively or defensively).

If the other person has to ask why you aren't doing what you said you would do, you are now on the defensive and have to explain your reasoning – which is never a position of strength – even if you have a very good reason. And, even if your explanations are good, you have unwittingly signaled that you are not the trusted advisor because the constituent had to ask you for your excuse; you didn't anticipate and offer it. Your explanation was communicated reactively and not proactively. The takeaway is to get ahead of any unfortunate situation the moment you realize your ability to honor your commitments is in jeopardy. Alert those affected to the possibility that you may not meet your deadlines. The sooner you communicate your status, the more others will view you as a trusted advisor.

4.3 Approachability and Credibility

There's one other trait that makes it easier for people to trust you – assuming your actions have established yourself as believable and reliable. That trait is your approachability. In other words, how easy is it for people to talk to you? The more people feel that you are easy to talk to, the more they will trust you – assuming again that your behavior is credible and dependable.

Have you ever been in a situation where you met someone new – maybe you were at a conference or on a plane – and you found this person so easy to talk to, as if you have known this person for a long time instead of just a few minutes or hours? If so, this person displayed approachability.

Now, at some other level, this person probably also displayed credibility to you (e.g., information you exchanged during small talk was accurate or believable) and reliability (i.e., common values or interests, shared experiences). Maybe the other person's executive presence telegraphed these perceptions to you.

In contrast, think about a person you have worked with and known for years but really don't know at all. When you reflect on your conversations with this person, you realize that the most you have discussed is the weather (too hot in the summer and too cold in the winter). You really don't know anything meaningful about this person (do they have kids, pets, hobbies?). I am not suggesting that you need to be on intimate social terms with everyone with whom you work. I am suggesting that if you can't easily talk to a person about superficial things, how can you discuss "trusted advisor" topics with this person?

HOW TO KEEP A CONVERSATION GOING

1. Once the other person answers your conversation-starting question, pause for 5–10 seconds. This has a couple of advantages. It subtly encourages your participant to embellish or expand on the response. It enables you to think about the response and ask appropriate follow-up questions.
2. Walk the talk and model the behavior you want the other person to demonstrate. Establish and maintain an open body position. Provide context for your questions so the participant understands the rationale for your questions.
3. Identify and expand on commonalities that you share with the other person to help the other person perceive you as a three-dimensional, whole person and not just someone who has a project or audit to complete.

Now, I realize that small talk comes easier to some people than it does to others. If you would like to increase your ability to make meaningful small talk – an important step to building the trusted advisor relationship – be prepared to discuss several interests or experiences. Ask yourself:

- What have I read lately that I enjoyed or found thought-provoking?
- What movie, play, or performance tickled my funny bone or captured my imagination?
- What restaurants could I recommend to someone who shares my tastes in food?
- What recordings or concerts have I heard that may interest other music lovers?
- Where have I traveled that exceeded my expectations?
- What new challenges am I setting for myself?
- What are my current hobbies?
- What plans do I have for this weekend or over the next holiday?
- What insights can I share about my business or work that might be interesting?

Notice that all of these questions are open-ended ones, intended to get the other person talking. Be prepared to prime the conversational pump by volunteering your answer to the question first – particularly if you are trying to make small talk with someone who is analytical. Just remember to keep your answer short and focus on hearing the other person's answer.

4.4 How We Undermine or Sabotage Ourselves

IS IT MICROMANAGING OR JUST THAT I DON'T BELIEVE YOU ANYMORE?

As a manager, I, like others, rely on information from my team members to make decisions. The information they supply becomes even more important because I travel and am not co-located with them.

My on-the-road routine is to have end-of-day reports from my team members (which are kind of like the agile daily meetings). Based on this information I can determine whether we are on course or priorities and team member tasks need to shift. These end-of-day meetings also enable me and individual team members to discuss anything new that has come up and to exchange ideas on planned or in-progress projects. These meetings could last for 10–30 minutes, depending on the agenda.

One of my former team members would provide brief summaries concerning progress and problems. For example, she might say, "I am working on client ABC's workbook or I am putting the PowerPoint together for client XYZ." And, she would provide quick answers to my follow-up questions.

While I appreciated the brevity – particularly at the day's end when I and everyone else are tired and ready to switch off to relax, I started to notice during subsequent conversations that she would correct information she had provided. Essentially, her brevity during end-of-day meetings had a price. Whenever she provided updated or corrected information, I noticed that we would spend at least as much time on the topic as we had when we originally discussed it. So, any time savings that we experienced because of the brief initial report were erased by the time spent in successive ones.

Had this happened once or twice, I would probably have never noticed. The more we had to revisit and change project statuses, the more I started to listen to the end-of-day reports with professional skepticism. Unconsciously, I began to expect inaccuracies in the report…and by extension doubted the person providing the information.

This situation was exacerbated by my professional style, which thrives on crossing things off the list and accomplishing things. Consequently, I felt frustrated whenever we needed to revisit and change decisions we had made. So, I started to ask follow-up questions to elicit the details I needed during brief end-of-day reports. My change in behavior had an unintended consequence: it was perceived as micromanaging.

After a couple of weeks of increasingly uncomfortable end-of-day reports, we finally talked things out and worked out a solution.

From listening to her, I learned that that she eliminated some of the details thinking they were unimportant – and from her perspective maybe they were. But those details were important to me because I viewed some of the situations from a different perspective (e.g., focusing on strategic or long-term implications). This difference in perspective affected her end-of-day meeting content.

I also had an important takeaway from this experience. My perception of this person was affected by my loss of trust in the accuracy of her reports. Essentially, I stopped seeing her as credible and instead, felt the need to gain assurance that her information was complete and accurate – a behavior that she viewed as micromanaging.

So if you feel that your manager is micromanaging you, is that really the case or is it that this person needs assurance that your work is complete and accurate?

Even though we realize the importance of being the trusted advisor, sometimes we inadvertently undermine ourselves. Essentially, we create our own hindrances. This self-sabotage can happen so quickly, often without us realizing that it has happened. Let me give you a couple of examples.

- If crossing things off the list provides you with a terrific sense of achievement, you may provide your manager and your constituents with answers too quickly. Take the time to pause and reflect on the completeness and accuracy of your data before providing information that will be quoted and used in decision-making. Also, take a pause to restate the question you are being asked to make sure you understand what the other person wants to know or how this person wants to use the information before you provide it.
- If you like to keep things simple, you may unwittingly be providing your manager and your constituents with incomplete information. Pay attention to the role and responsibilities of the person asking the question. Are you providing overview level answers to people who need information at a tactical level? If so, this dearth of data will come back to haunt you.
- If you typically tell people how to build the clock when they ask what time it is, you may leave others with the perception that things are more complicated than they actually are. Focus on whether the person asking the question is in a senior level role and looking for a summary, big picture perspective.

"We need people in our lives with whom we can be as open as possible. To have real conversations with people may seem like such a simple, obvious suggestion, but it involves courage and risk."

Thomas Moore

an American psychotherapist, former monk, and author

4.5 Why Being a Trusted Advisor Is So Important

In case it is not crystal clear by now, you need to be perceived as a trusted advisor by others if you want them to feel comfortable discussing tough situations with you. Stop and think about the topics you need to discuss during audit planning, inherent risk assessment discussions, walk-throughs, control effectiveness testing, and status meeting. You are typically asking about vulnerabilities:

- What are the strategic or longer-range concerns you have about your process or entity's future?
- What could go wrong to threaten the achievement of your business objective?
- What are known gaps or problems with your workflow or control design and operation?

From a practical perspective, if you were being audited, you wouldn't want to discuss any of these things unless you trusted the person with whom you were speaking. And, if you had to answer these questions and you didn't know or trust the interviewer, your answers would be brief. You would provide no more – and probably less – than you were asked.

Consequently, you need others to trust you if you are going to do a good job. And, when others trust you, obtaining the information you need to do your job is considerably easier.

For Skill Practice

1. People will trust you if you are credible, reliable, and approachable. What specific things can you do or say during conversations and meetings that will communicate credibility, accuracy, knowledge, and experience to others? What specific things can you do or say that will let others know that they can rely and depend on you? What specific things can you do or say that will make it easier for others to approach you and talk to you?

2. If you are wondering how to increase your approachability, make a conscious effort to display the following actions from now on:
   - Be sincere.
   - Search for individuals who seem receptive.
   - Establish eye contact and smile to send receptive signals. (Eye contact for 5 to 10 seconds indicates curiosity and is generally considered friendly. Take care not to stare

at another person too intensely though because this can make him or her feel uncomfortable.)

- Be the first to introduce yourself and ask an easy, open-ended question.
- Listen carefully for facts, feelings, and key words.
- Highlight mutual interests.

Chapter Summary

- To be your constituents' trusted advisor, you need to be honest, dependable, and approachable.
- The more people feel that you are easy to talk to, the more they will trust you (assuming that your information is accurate and your behavior is consistent).
- Being perceived as a trusted advisor will help you when you need to discuss anything and everything at any stage of a project or audit.

My Takeaway Game Plan

My Goal is:

Behaviors I will *start* to achieve my goal...

Behaviors I will *continue* to achieve my goal...

Behaviors I will *stop* to achieve my goal...

Leading and Lagging Indicators – How I'll Measure My Results

5

INFLUENCING OTHERS FOR RESULTS

Think twice before you speak because your words and influence will plant the seed of either success or failure in the mind of another.

Napoleon Hill

American Self-help Author of Think and Grow Rich and The Law of Success

When you think of influential people, who comes to mind? And, more importantly, how do you feel about them? For example, do you think of people that you admire (like a favorite teacher or mentor-like boss) and would like to emulate? Or, do you think of the proverbial high-pressure-tactics sales person, who will do or say anything to get you to sign on the dotted line and make a purchase? I ask because your attitude toward influence affects your ability.

If you value the ability to influence, then you want to gain the skills needed to do it effectively. In contrast, if you believe that influencers are manipulators who are only interested in satisfying their own selfish agendas, you would not want to acquire any influential ability.

Technically, influence is *the act or power of producing an effect without apparent exertion of force or direct exercise of command*[1]. You can be influenced by peers, friends, and other people – even those you do not know personally. If you don't believe me, consider the effect of advertising on consumer behavior, or the highly profitable social media influencers who peddle credible (and sometimes, somewhat dubious) products and services.

But, if you report to me and I tell you to do something and you do it, I didn't influence you. I gave you a work assignment. You acted in response to my request because I am your manager, not because I was influential. Generally, when a manager asks a direct report to do something, the manager is acting within his or her role as a boss, not as a colleague or peer, who is making a suggestion. That said, you may work for a manager who communicates in such a persuasive way that you can't wait to start the assignment. If this is the case, your manager may be using some of the influencing techniques that I want to share with you. Having an influential manager just makes you more eager to do the work – it doesn't change the fact that you are responsible to accomplish what you were assigned to do.

5.1 Is Influence Just a Manipulation?

According to Merriam Webster's Dictionary[2], "manipulation" has a couple of meanings. One meaning is to "manage or utilize skillfully." Another meaning is "to control or play upon by artful, unfair, or insidious means especially to one's own advantage." When you think about the word "*manipulate*" which meaning comes to mind – the neutral one or the negative one?

Fundamentally, all influence is a manipulation because it produces an effect in someone else's behavior without pulling rank or coercing the other person into action. Influencers are able to persuade others to take an action the influencer wants – essentially controlling others' behavior. Whether the influencer's result is positive or negative depends on the nature of the effect produced and the ethics of the performer and influencer.

IT'S JUST A MEAL

Muffy and Ishkabiddle have been coworkers for years and enjoy lunch together several times a week. They alternate choosing the lunch restaurant. Muffy likes to try new places and Ishkabiddle enjoys frequenting the same places and becoming a "regular."

Every time they go to a familiar restaurant – which they do at least once a week – Ishkabiddle orders the same meal. One day, Muffy suggests that Ishkabiddle order something different from the menu. "I know you were at this restaurant earlier in the week, ordered your favorite meal, and still have leftovers in the office refrigerator to prove it," says Muffy. She points out that there are other dishes on the menu with ingredients like the ones in Ishkabiddle's favorite dish and these entrees are the same price (or less) than the cost of Ishkabiddle's favorite meal. Muffy adds, "You have been enjoying this chef's food for a number of years, consequently, you know it is consistently tasty." "Wouldn't it be nice to have a back-up plan in case your favorite meal isn't on the menu one day?"

Muffy also suggests, "Life is short; why not try something new and be a little creative. Besides, this is just one meal – you can always return to ordering your favorite meal the next time." After listening to the points Muffy has raised, Ishkabiddle decides to order something different from the menu. He's been influenced.

For this book's purpose, I am making the assumption that our motivation for influencing others is positive. You and I want to create value. We want to see measurable improvements in our organization's risk management culture. We want to make it easier for our business colleagues to make sound short- and long-term decisions, particularly during times of uncertainty. We want to enable our constituents to enact and enforce policies that are ethical, consistent, and compliant with regulations.

All of the influencing techniques are deliberately intended to change or motivate another person's behavior – to get this person to start, stop, or continue doing something that you want done. The techniques, per se, have neither positive nor negative intent.

If you feel that I am twisting your arm to take action, I am not engaged in influence. I am coercing you. The minute I stop forcing you to act, you will stop because you were not convinced, just bullied. Admittedly, the line between reminding you about your fears and engaging you in intimidation tactics is thin.

You can be much more influential if people are not aware of your influence.

Unknown

5.2 What Are the Traits of an Effective Influencer?

In your heart of hearts, do you question the need to influence others because you believe that the facts concerning risks, control gaps, design flaws, and execution errors should be enough to motivate corrective action? Do you find it challenging to influence others and demonstrate the behaviors of influential people? Is it difficult or time-consuming to come up with various ways to express the same idea?

If so, you may prefer to think critically and analytically instead of thinking heuristically and creatively. While I am not suggesting that you sacrifice or reduce your critical thinking (because it is a core audit competency), the ability to persuade or influence can be useful at various points during a project or review.

It can be challenging to shift from demonstrating critical thinking behavior to influencer behavior because critical thinking is the antithesis of influencing. Essentially, when you think critically (i.e., analyzing, evaluating, logical reasoning) you use skills that are oppositional to those used to influence others (i.e., persuading, convincing, motivating).

Influencing is the act of persuading others to see a certain point of view or change an existing attitude.

Critical thinking is an inward process that helps you deduce information from verbal and nonverbal communication.

Influencers.....	Critical Thinkers.....
Use general terms (e.g., most, usually, typically, everyone, no one).	Use specific terms and cite specific amounts.
Emphasize data related to shared values and commonalities.	Focus on all data objectively and equally.

Effective influencers demonstrate the following behaviors:

- Broad-based appeal – This is the ability to understand and be understood by a diversified array of individuals. This array could span role, ranks, or title within an organization, department, or team. It could span ages and generations. It could span corporate cultures that range from command-control environments to ones that are highly participatory and democratic. The person who possesses broad-based appeal is comfortable and effective in communicating with anyone at any time about anything.

Broad-based appeal means that you are capable of engaging in a bidirectional communication: you are able to *understand the other person* (regardless of this person's role, experience, and relationship to you) and you communicate in a way that *makes it easy for the other person to understand you.* This understanding goes beyond simply hearing the words that are said. It includes the ability to appreciate the speaker's meaning as well (i.e., is the person communicating sarcasm or sincerity and tentativeness or confidence) based on the tone of voice and vocal inflection. It also includes acknowledging and appreciating the context for the person's message (e.g., is the speaker experienced or new in his or her role, is the situation routine or unprecedented). All of these factors affected the speaker's message and how you interpret and understand it.

To demonstrate broad-based appeal, you must be able to empathize with others. Empathy is the crucial component and it is not the same thing as sympathy. Sympathy means that you feel sad or sorry for another person's situation or predicament. Sympathy is about you and your reactions to another person's situation or message.

Empathy means that you can see the world through the other person's eyes and understand it without judging it. Empathy enables you to appreciate or value the other person's perspective and feelings although they may be very different from your own. Of all the traits that comprise influence, in my view, empathy is the most important one because it enables you to understand the other person's motivation, raison d'etre, and rationale.

Demonstrating empathy implies having an other-directedness that enables you to suspend your own perspective, opinions, and ideas, while you clear your mind and leave it open to nonjudgmentally receive the message the other person is sending. When you empathize, you actively engage in making sure that you have heard and understood the other person's message.

Admittedly, being empathetic is easier said than done. As auditors and risk professionals, we get paid to conclude and give our opinions. It may be helpful to view empathy as the ability to acquire information from others that has not been affected by our thoughts and opinions. The more empathic you are, the more you will be able to obtain information from others that is not unwittingly biased by your own experience and mental filters. Viewed this way, being empathetic enables you to collect complete information more effectively. When I find myself jumping to judge, I find it helpful to remember that I will have plenty of time to think critically and evaluate the message at a later point during the project.

- Emotional intelligence – This is the ability to demonstrate self-awareness and self-control while simultaneously demonstrating an awareness of others' needs and managing productive relationships with them.
- Verbal agility – This is the ability to say the same thing in many different ways. Admittedly, having a well-developed vocabulary is a prerequisite for this capability. If you only have one way to express your ideas or rationale, it will be difficult to express nuanced or complex concepts or issues.

Equally important, having this ability means that you can express yourself in ways that enable others to understand your message. You are able to choose the right word that conveys your meaning. When you have verbal agility, you can immediately restate your message in different terms as soon as you notice the start of a potential misunderstanding or an undesired reaction from the other person. You can verbally pivot and keep the exchange productive.

If you are wondering whether you have verbal agility, take the challenge.

HOW VERBALLY AGILE ARE YOU?

Before taking this exercise, set a clock timer to 7 minutes. As the clock counts down, list as many synonyms and synonymous expressions (i.e., phrases or sentences) that come to mind for each of the words below. Ready? Go!

Risk

Control

Finding

Exception

Standard

Impact

Likelihood

- Credibility – This trait was initially described in Unit 4 as a component of trustworthiness. Unsurprisingly, people are influenced by those they trust. If a complete stranger walked up to you or called you and began recommending that you take certain actions, you would probably either walk away or hang up without a second thought. The idea of acting on suggestions from those you don't know or trust is preposterous.

    You may trust someone as a result of direct personal knowledge or experience of this individual (i.e., you have worked with them and know that this person is honest and factual when providing information) or you may trust the organization with which this person is affiliated (i.e., the company has a reputation for making ethical business decisions, acting fairly with suppliers and employees, and providing quality data, products, or services). You may also trust another person because this person was recommended to you by someone else who you know and trust (which is also called affinity marketing). Networking is the basis for affinity marketing and functions on the premise that "birds of a feather flock together" (i.e., people with shared values associate with each other).

The following behaviors contribute to your ability to project credibility:

- Experience (particularly when it has been successful – although negative or bad experiences can be influential in terms of what not to do).
- Accuracy and completeness in the data you provide.
- Balance in terms of the perspective or context you provide, particularly when you cite test results or describe audit findings. For example, citing a 10% error rate without specifying whether the context is the total population or just the items you sampled completely changes the message. And, if the person receiving this information has to ask you for the contextual data, you risk appearing defensive when you provide it.
- Preparedness – According to the adage, luck favors the prepared mind. The more you can anticipate the other person's needs and values, the more you will be able to come up with the approach and word choice you need to be persuasive. Being prepared also means that you have thought through a "Plan B" and "Plan C" in the event that your initial approach meets resistance. Although Chapter 9 discusses how to overcome objections in detail, the point now is that you need to be ready to shift approaches if you encounter pushback or some of the assumptions you used to plan your approach turn out to be wrong.
- Shared values – These are the beliefs, norms, and philosophies that are elemental or core to an individual's decision-making. These values encompass what is right or wrong, what is appropriate or inappropriate behavior, what is considered attractive or unattractive. The source of one's values are myriad, beginning with family, and expanding to include education and life experiences. The more you can display or communicate that you share values with the person you are trying to persuade, the more influential you will be.

5.3 Are You a Pusher or a Puller When It Comes to Influencing Others?

If you aren't sure whether you are a pusher or puller, consider your typical behavior when you are trying to persuade another person to take action.

If you spend most of your time talking and giving examples or offering additional support for your message, you are a pusher. If you spend most of your time asking questions of those you are trying to influence, you are a puller. Which is better? Well, that depends on you, the other person, and the situation.

Push techniques are those where you act directly by:

- Stating what you want. This means clarifying your requirements (e.g., "I need…, I want…").
- Expressing views and opinions by giving information, making suggestions, using facts to build a case, making judgments (e.g., "I suggest…, I recommend…").
- Expressing feelings by telling others the effect of their behavior on the situation (e.g., "When people shout, I don't respond well.").
- Using pressures and incentives by offering inducements, cajoling, pressuring, counter arguing (e.g., "If you do…, I will…").

Pull techniques are those where you consider the other person's point of view by:

- Actively listening (e.g., using "uh-huhs," paraphrasing what the other person has said, checking understanding).
- Encouraging and questioning by asking for the other person's opinion, using open questions to gather information (e.g., "Tell me what you think").
- Being open to another's suggestions. This means empathizing and seeing things from the other person's viewpoint (e.g., "So you would like that?").
- Building and supporting the common ground. This means building on suggestions, finding common ground, reaching consensus, showing agreement (e.g., "I agree with what Muffy says").
- Nodding while the other person speaks to encourage the speaker to continue.

In *It's Just a Meal*, Muffy was engaged in pushing. Although she asked Ishkabiddle a couple of questions (which is typically a "pull" indicator), she didn't wait for a response (which is typical push behavior).

Essentially, Muffy's questions were rhetorical and not intended to get Ishkabiddle talking and elicit information about his reasons for ordering the same meal.

To influence effectively, you need to use a balance of "push" and "pull" techniques. You may be wondering how you will know when to push and when to pull. The answer to this question depends on what is happening during the conversation and your behavior during it.

Focus on your behavior because it is the only thing you can control. Have you been speaking or providing information? If so, you have been pushing. Ask yourself whether the other person seems convinced and eager to act. If both conditions are met, you are successful. If not, you have not been completely successful in your influencing efforts. You need to switch tactics and actively start pulling. Do this by asking open-ended questions that will encourage the others involved to discuss the things they like and do not like about the suggestion or corrective action under discussion.

Have you have been listening more than you have been talking and have you been asking questions to elicit information from the person or people you are trying to influence? Do they seem convinced and eager to act? If so, you were successful. If not, you need to switch your behavior and begin pushing. Provide examples and supporting information to address their concerns and objections.

By the way, you will know you have been successful in influencing when the other side asks you implementation-oriented questions like, "What's the next step?" or they begin to talk about details associated with actually doing whatever you are discussing. The more the other side indicates that they can imagine the suggestion or corrective action in place, the more you know you were persuasive.

5.4 What Influences Others to Act?

If you have ever studied management theory, you are familiar with Abraham Maslow's *Hierarchy of Needs*, which is typically depicted as a triangular diagram that has basic survival needs at the base (food, shelter) and self-actualization (realizing your potential and being all you can) at the triangle's tip. In between survival and self-actualization are safety, affiliation with others, and esteem. Published in 1943, it is an explanation of the five categories of things that motivate human behavior. While others have leveraged and expanded on Maslow's model, I think it provides good starting point for understanding how to influence others.

One starting point for influencing others is to understand their situation. For example, if the other person is wondering how to generate the income needed to keep the business or project viable, you need to position your ideas in ways that clearly show they will address this need and generate income. Confine your ideas to ones that directly address this immediate need.

Most people want to acquire more benefits and results that are pleasurable (also known as carrots) and they want to avoid anything that could lead to loss, pain, or discomfort (also known as sticks). So, when coming up with your message, identify the carrots and sticks that will resonate with the person you want to influence.

For example, most business people want to achieve their business objectives, largely because they want to keep their jobs and earn incentive compensation for exceeding goals. Any of your ideas that will help the other person achieve this would be perceived as a carrot or good thing and would influence the other person to act. Most business people do not want to go to jail (the exception being those that work in correctional facilities). Consequently, you may want to point out how taking corrective action could enable the business person to do the right thing and comply with regulations and policies.

Another way to influence others at work is to focus on existing and desired business relationships. For example, most people want to please their boss and the members of the executive team. Why? They want to continue to be employed (security needs); they want to be valued (esteem and belonging); they want to be promoted (self-actualization); and they want to take time-tested action. So, when you are discussing your ideas or corrective action, depending on the situation, you might want to point out that:

- The corrective action will make it easier for them to accomplish their objective.
- The executives support the recommended action.
- Other departments (or competitors or the industry leaders) have implemented the corrected action with favorable results.
- The corrective action will comply with regulations and avoid the potential of fines and sanctions.

You can influence others by understanding their thinking style. Is the other person's thinking systematic or heuristic? The systematic mode refers to a person who is carefully and consciously thinking. The thought process is active, creative, and alert. It may come across as logical, sequenced, or patterned. The heuristic mode, by contrast, is at the other extreme of thinking. Here the person is not really thinking very carefully and instead is skimming along the surface of ideas. The thinking is enough to be aware of the situation, but not carefully enough to catch flaws, errors, and inconsistencies in the situation. Heuristic thinking may come across as high-level, random, or unsequenced.

While some people are flexible in their thinking and can move back and forth between the two modes, balancing their thinking and emotional responses depending on the situation, others have a strong individual preference for a particular thinking mode and can only process information by using it. For example, extremely systematic thinkers tend to number items in a list and will not deviate from the numbered order when discussing them. In contrast extreme heuristic thinkers may not even have a list! Or, the items in the list may not be sequenced or if sequenced, may not be covered in the listed order.

Systematic thinkers have a high need for cognition and think carefully and analytically about the decisions they need to make or how they will handle the situations they face (e.g., let's study it, let's ask more questions, let's get more data). By contrast heuristic thinkers have a low need for cognition and typically think consciously as little as possible about a decision or situation, preferring instead to pick up, interpret, and respond to nonverbal cues and clues (e.g., changes in rate of speech, word choice, and phrasing), and other situational factors (e.g., precedents, how others will react, the internal political climate). Heuristic thinkers act on their intuition, prior experience, and internal reaction. They are quite comfortable trusting their "gut feeling" because it is the response to all of their compressed memories of their life experience that have been triggered by the current decision or situation they need to handle.

When people are in the systematic mode, certain factors, called "arguments," will be very important and influential to them. The systematic thinker will be looking for facts, evidence, examples, reasoning, consistency, and logic.

By contrast, when people are in the heuristic mode, other things will be important. Since arguments (i.e., facts, evidence, reasoning, etc.) require a lot of cognitive effort and energy, the heuristic thinker won't use them very much. Qualitative or subjective factors like the attractiveness, friendliness, or expertise of the source will be more influential for the heuristic thinker. These factors are called "cues."

When people are influenced while thinking systematically, the influence is more likely to stick precisely because the people thought about it more carefully, fully, and deeply. For heuristic thinkers, however, any influence is likely to be rather short lived, simply because they did not really think that much.

The key to choosing the right approach is empathy, which is why it is an essential trait for influencers. Do not project your assumptions of what is important to the other person. Take the time to do your homework and leverage the insights of other members of your team. You want to make sure that influencing approach is relevant, realistic, and sincere. If it seems hackneyed or exaggerated, it will not work. And, your credibility will be impugned, which will reduce your executive presence, influencing ability, and perceived value as a trusted advisor.

> There are two parts to influence: First, influence is powerful; and second, influence is subtle. You wouldn't let someone push you off course, but you might let someone nudge you off course and not even realize it.
>
> **Jim Rohn, Author, Motivational speaker**

5.5 Strategies for Increased Influencing Ability

Take the following actions to increase your ability to influence others:

- Increase your empathy by spending a couple of minutes imagining how the other person is viewing the world. Consider their objectives as well as the concerns or reservations they may have. How familiar are they with what you want to discuss with them? How often have they had to make the type of decision you want them to make?
- Identify and determine the other person's preferred mental mode, (i.e., systematic or heuristic), by observing the non-verbal behaviors and listening to the way the other person

responds to the questions you ask. Specifically, notice whether the other person's response sounds sequenced, detailed, specific, which indicates systematic thinking, or randomly organized and general, which indicates heuristic thinking. If you are not sure about the other person's preferred thinking mode, the rationale for your idea should appeal to both.

If you have the opportunity to meet with the other person more than once, consider the questions the other person asks: Is there a pattern or predictability to the nature or order of the questions? If so, this may indicate a systematic thinker. Does the person bring up or ask about different, seemingly unrelated to the topic under discussion? If so, this could indicate a heuristic thinker.

- Communicate how your suggestion or idea is consistent with what has been done in similar situations in the past because breaking with traditional is typically viewed as risky. You want to show or provide support that indicates that the proposed decision will be aligned with what has been done in the past. If what you are suggesting is a departure from the precedent, you need to communicate that what has been done in the past is no longer the most effective response to the current situation.

- Be instrumental in defining the roles of others and creating frameworks for accomplishing results. Although you may have made a persuasive suggestion, people may not take action because the decision-making process is unclear – particularly if your suggestion is a novel one (i.e., no precedent exists). By remembering to ask questions like, "Who needs to sign off on this" or "What is the decision-making process for something like this?" you enable others to focus on the steps they need to take to convert an idea into action. If you work in a matrix organization, in which individuals may answer to multiple bosses, getting answers to these questions are essential if you want to achieve results.

- Develop a track record for arriving at fair and equitable, "win-win" solutions for risk management challenges or dilemmas. You can do this by fostering climates of open exchange of information among all parties that are involved, so that they are comfortable describing their reservations and concerns. By understanding each party's goals and concerns, you can help the group come up with viable solutions.

- Expand your vocabulary so that you are able to say the same thing in many different ways. Use words that are simple, yet clearly explain your message. Keep your sentences short because they will be easier to understand during a phone call or in an email.

- Demonstrate values and behaviors that are congruent with the corporate culture and those who are at the meeting. Strive to walk the talk so that your behaviors demonstrate your values – particularly in a digital business environment in which people see your emails before they may see you in person. Documents that contain errors or misspellings telegraph your values in a more memorable way than your spoken words.

Nothing has a greater influence over your life than your thoughts whether they are negative or positive.

Tasha Hoggatt
Author of What Makes You Great?

5.6 Are You Sabotaging Yourself?

You may be undermining your influencing ability without even realizing it by sending a mixed message to the person you are trying to persuade. Which of the following expressions have you ever used?

- From an audit perspective…
- From a corporate (enterprise or home office) perspective…
- This may seem like an ignorant (or silly) question but…
- This may not work but…
- I'm not sure you want to do this.

Each of these expressions may seem innocent, but each one undermines the influence you are trying to build. The first two are divisive, which is the antithesis of demonstrating shared values. If you are talking to other auditors, then it is perfectly fine to say, "From an audit perspective." And, if you are in the company of other corporate staffers, then it is fine to say "from a corporate perspective." If not, then all you have accomplished is to remind the other person of the differences (not the similarities) you share. Remember that people like people who are like themselves. Consequently, for maximum influence you want to remind the people you want to influence of all the similarities you have – not the number of differences that exist.

The next three expressions plant seeds of negative ideas or feelings in the mind of the person you are trying to influence right before you describe your suggestion or recommendation. These phrases may be intended to soften your ideas and make them more palatable but they have quite the opposite effect. They engender negativity and enable the listener to associate this negativity with you and your ideas. Think about it. Who would intentionally ask a silly question and waste everyone's time? All new ideas are risky and may not work but why preface your suggestion by reminding everyone that your idea could fail?

Stop sabotaging yourself. Just suppress the audio on these and other similar expressions. They add no value and in fact, detract from your message. Instead, simply express your idea and show how your idea will help the other person achieve their objective.

For Skill Practice

1. If you are wondering how to increase your ability to influence others, you can take the following actions:
    - Pay attention to the typical ways you try to influence others. Then, focus on whether these methods are working. Are you getting others to agree with your point of view? Or, do people initially agree and then change their minds and back away from these agreements at a later date. If the latter happens, they were probably not completely convinced. Or, perhaps the value, benefit, or consequence you described was not particularly meaningful to them.
    - When trying to influence others, it is always good to have a backup plan. In how many different ways can you express the same message?
    - How does your message change when you are trying to influence a business leader, department head, or executive compared to when you are trying to influence a peer?

Think about how you prepare to influence these different types of people. Do you use the same approach to persuade or a different one based on the person you are trying to influence?

2. Think about the last three times you were trying to influence someone else. How did things turn out in each situation – were you successful?
   - Were you pushing or pulling to make your points?
   - If you used both techniques, which one did you use first or more often (i.e., your preferred style)?
   - Were you comfortable switching from a pull to a push strategy and vice versa?
   - If you only used one style and it didn't work, how will you remember to recognize this situation and switch styles?

3. Recall the last three important business decisions you had to make. What factors affected your decision (e.g., cost, precedents, fairness, historic practice)?

4. If you are a member of a management team or board, consider the last three business decisions the group has made. What factors affected those decisions? How do these factors compare to the ones you prefer to use? If there are differences, would it be useful to add the additional factors to the decision criteria you already use? If yes, how will you remember to consider these additional factors when making decisions?

Chapter Summary

- Whether influence is positive or negative depends on one's motivation as well as the nature of the change you want to achieve. Are you trying to bring about a self-serving or capricious behavioral change in others or are you trying to achieve a greater, ethical, organizational good? Either way, the techniques will be the same and will work because they appeal to human nature and the factors that affect how individuals make decisions.
- However, if you are an effective influencer, the other person will feel good about taking the action that you suggest.

- When planning how you will influence others, be sure you understand their needs and goals and that this information is not biased by your own experience and mental filters.
- The more the other side indicates that they can imagine the suggestion or corrective action in place and operating, the more you know you were persuasive.

Notes

1 Merriam-Webster online Dictionary; https://www.merriam-webster.com/dictionary/influence
2 Merriam-Webster

My Takeaway Game Plan

My Goal is:

Behaviors I will *start* to achieve my goal...

Behaviors I will *continue* to achieve my goal...

Behaviors I will *stop* to achieve my goal...

Leading and Lagging Indicators – How I'll Measure My Results

6

FACILITATING MEETINGS AND DISCUSSIONS

> You have a meeting to make a decision, not to decide on the question.
>
> **Bill Gates**
>
> *co-founder of Microsoft, an American business magnate,*
> *software developer, investor, and philanthropist.*

It is not easy to follow Bill Gates' advice. Thanks to the general ability to work from home, combined with globalism, the people you need to collaborate with may be in different countries, time zones, or locations – any place other than the same work space you are in. Consequently, you cannot count on impromptu conversations and discussions to obtain the information or answer you need or to provide status updates and exchange ideas.

Instead, you need to either set up a standing, recurring meeting (which is fine if the other people are members of the same project team you are in) or you need to send a meeting invitation to have a conversation with another person. And, based on the outcome of this conversation, you may decide that you need to convene another conversation, which really is a meeting. Either way, these discussions need to be scheduled in advance and require some preparation. The preparation is important because you may have to wait a week (or more depending on the other person's role and responsibilities) just to identify a mutually convenient meeting date and time to start the conversation.

DOI: 10.1201/9781003093978-6

THE THREE-PHASE MEETING PROCESS

PHASE 1: PLANNING FOR THE INTERVIEW: DO YOUR HOMEWORK FIRST	PHASE 2: SETTING THE INTERVIEW CLIMATE AND POSING THE QUESTIONS	PHASE 3: CLOSING THE INTERVIEW AND VERIFYING MUTUAL UNDERSTANDING
• Determine your objectives. • Understand your participant's organization, organizational role, and communication style by reviewing existing material and talking with others in your department. • Formulate the areas you wish to cover. • Reality check your questions to make sure they will accomplish your interview objective. • Create an agenda.	• Break the ice and establish rapport. • Create a framework for the interview by explaining the purpose of the interview as it relates to the audit, using terms that the participant understands. • Verify that the participant understands the interview's purpose. • Use the appropriate combination of interviewing tools (e.g., The Funnel Approach and probes). • Listen to what the participant has to say. • Take notes to record key information. • Stay on schedule – watch the time!	• Use restatement to confirm your understanding of the participant's responses and key points. • Ask participants to restate or summarize their responses. • Provide feedback to the participant concerning how the interview went. • Review the open items and reach agreement on the steps needed to resolve them. • Wrap up the interview by recapping your understanding of what's been communicated.

And, when you actually have your voice-to-voice or (virtual) face-to-face time, you want to make it as productive as possible. Depending on where you are in the audit process, you want to be sure to cover all the topics you need to complete your planning, discuss all the possible reasons a control gap, design flaw, or execution error could occur, and get the other person's input concerning all corrective actions because it will probably take two more weeks before you can meet again. If you want to be able to deliver your audit deliverables on time, your meetings have to be well planned and well executed.

6.1 Why Meet at All?

Meetings move at the speed of the slowest mind in the room.

Dale Alan Dauten

American business management columnist, author,
professional speaker, management coach, and mediator

Dale Dauten's quote might not sound like an endorsement for meetings. According to John Kenneth Galbraith, a Canadian-American economist, public official, and diplomat: *"Meetings are indispensable when you don't want to do anything."* Pawan Mishra, an award-winning author, producer, director, and a leader in finance and technology industries described a meeting as "a collective tacit confession of participants' unwillingness to work." "A meeting consists of a group of people who have little to say – until after the meeting" according to P.K. Shaw, author.

Why do meetings evoke such pessimism and sarcasm? Probably because these sentiments are grounded in experience and have a seed of truth.

Let's face it, many meetings are not productive. Think about the number of times you have been at a meeting and wondered why you were invited. Think about the outcomes of recent meetings you have had. What percentage of these meetings has resulted in another meeting instead of an actionable decision? In both these cases, your time (and maybe others' time as well) could have been put to better use.

QUESTIONS TO ASK BEFORE AND AFTER MEETINGS

Questions to ask yourself before going to a meeting:
- Why am I going?
- Who do I want to meet?
- What do I expect to accomplish?

Questions to ask yourself upon returning:
- Did I stick to my plan?
- How did I accomplish my goals?
- What can/should I do differently next time?
- What follow-up action do I need to take with the people I met?

6.2 To Meet or Not to Meet, That Is the Question

Before scheduling a meeting, determine whether you need one at all. What information do you need? Do you need background or historic information, which can be obtained through research and reading, or do you need to collaborate with another person? Do you need the answer to a simple question or uncomplicated situation? If so, send an email to the person who can answer your question – no meeting necessary.

If you think you need a meeting, answer the following questions:

- What will the meeting achieve (i.e., how will things be different after the meeting; what will be decided or implemented)?
- Who are the *only* people that need to be at the meeting? The answer to this question is intended to limit the number of invitees to those who have a direct stake in the meeting objective or a speaking role during the meeting (i.e., some information to contribute that will enable the meeting objective's achievement).
- How much time will we need for this meeting? This answer is a function of the number of things you need to accomplish or the number of issues you need to discuss as well as the significance, novelty, or complexity of these issues. For example, you may only have one issue, but it is one with severe consequences or several ramifications. This single issue may require an entire hour (or more) to discuss and resolve.
- What information do the participants need to know *before* the meeting starts in order to be productive during it? Ideally, all participants should be on the same page at the meeting's start. Otherwise, you can waste time bringing some attendees up to speed while you are boring the other ones.
- When should the meeting be scheduled? The classic textbook answer to this question is to schedule the meeting when people are most alert and to avoid the afternoons before holidays and weekends (which is terrific advice if you could implement it). The practical answer is to schedule it when the key people are available. Consider when the meeting will occur for the majority of the participants and set the time accordingly. Of course, if each team member works in a different continent,

varying the meeting times for recurring meetings may be the fairest scheduling method. If you work for a global organization, be mindful that the time you set for the meeting will be different for the geographically dispersed participants (i.e., it may be early morning for some attendees while it is evening for others).

Luck is a matter of preparation meeting opportunity.

Lucius Annaeus Seneca
philosopher, statesman, orator, and tragedian

A CHECKLIST FOR PLANNING EFFECTIVE MEETINGS

To make sure that you will get the most from your meeting, ask yourself the following questions as you make your arrangements:

Will a meeting actually be useful and helpful in this case?

Are the right people going to be attending?

Has a clear agenda been prepared and distributed ahead of time?

Do you have all the supporting materials and supplies (i.e., any facts and figures gathered in preparation, as well as markers, flipcharts, tape, etc.)?

Has everyone been informed of the meeting's time and location?

Have participants carried out any assignments needed to prepare for the meeting?

Do all members of your team have speaking roles during the meeting?

6.3 Six Steps to Planning Effective Meetings

Once you have determined that you need a meeting, these steps will help you prepare to convene an effective one:

Step 1: Determine your goal. Is it to make a decision, provide a status update, educate, or persuade? Is the meeting topic or topics new or unprecedented (i.e., no one or only a few meeting attendees are familiar with the situation) or is the situation routine and fairly typical? The more unusual the situation, the more time the participants may need to understand and deal with it.

As you think about your meeting's purpose, you might find it helpful to work backward. Imagine that the meeting is over: What did you learn? What did you accomplish? The answers to these questions will make it easier for you to identify the topics you need to cover and the questions you need to ask.

Step 2: Identify the people who need to participate and consider where they will be at the time of the meeting (e.g., video, in person, phone, home office, work office, etc.). Given your meeting's goal and topics, consider whether the participants will have access to what they need to make decisions and take actions, or will you need to provide this information.

Consider what you know about the people who will attend the meeting. Plan in advance how you will encourage quiet or closed-mouthed participants to talk.

Step 3: Outline the key points or topics that need to be covered, including the meeting flow and who will speak first, second, etc., to create a high-level, initial agenda. (More on agendas later in this chapter.) Make sure the people who need to report on the various topics are available. Estimate the time each topic will require and communicate the time limits to everyone who will be present during the meeting.

Step 4: Prepare your notes and supporting documentation for the topics for which you are responsible. If you will not be the only person presenting information at the meeting, make sure the other participants are prepared to provide supporting documentation for their messages. For example, if your meeting's purpose is to provide status concerning an audit's or sprint's progress, make sure that you bring and are ready to share specific examples of your observations or results. This way, you can keep everyone engaged, focused, and productive. By showing examples, you make it easy to discuss what you found and its possible causes.

Step 5: Rehearse your message to make sure it fits within the time allocated and addresses the typical questions or reactions the other meeting participants will have. If the meeting is a high-profile one (e.g., a Town Hall or All Hands meeting), convene a dress rehearsal to make sure that the equipment and software work and that the supporting documentation is easy to read and understand.

Step 6: Open the phone or video line before the official meeting start time to give yourself time to get organized and ready to greet the attendees as they arrive. This approach makes it easier for you to keep track of people as they join the meeting. Assuming that you do not have a large group in attendance, you can use the pre-meeting time to break the ice with individuals as they join and set a conversational tone for the meeting.

Remember to start the meeting on time and follow the agenda.... assuming you created one. (Keep reading in case you haven't.) And, if you have only traded emails with the attendees, be sure to put each person at ease by smiling (if you are on video or in person), introducing yourself, and describing your position as well as the audit and meeting objectives. Be sure to communicate the meeting framework – a technique covered later in this chapter.

6.4 Do I Really Need an Agenda?

When I ask the auditors in my training sessions whether they use agendas, the response is quite mixed. In some departments, the auditors are required to use templated agendas that have been created for the opening meeting. These templates are intended to "script" the lead auditor and make it easier to remember to cover the various topics that need to be addressed at the start of an audit engagement.

If the project or audit will require recurring status meetings, it is helpful to set the meeting day and time at the project's start. This way, all team members will have the meeting time blocked on their calendars. (It is always easier to cancel a meeting than it is to schedule one.) At the same time, you set the recurring meeting date, set the standing agenda, which may be as simple as asking each project team member to provide a 5–10-minute summary concerning:

- What they are working on and have accomplished against their plan.
- The obstacles they have encountered that are blocking progress. (The intent is to describe the obstacle, not use the status

meeting to resolve it. A separate meeting should be set up for problem solving because different people may need to participate.)

- Whether they are able to move on to address the next item in their project plan or audit program.

Once an audit is underway in earnest, many auditors do not provide agendas to the meeting attendees, although they may have created one for their own use. In fact, some auditors don't use agendas at all. Instead, they start the meeting with just a purpose in mind (e.g., to gain an understanding of the process under review, to discuss the inherent risks in a process, or to understand how a particular control works).

Now, if the focus of the meeting is straightforward and uncomplicated, simply stating the meeting purpose is enough and you probably don't need a formal agenda – a working one will do. By working agenda, I am referring to the agenda that you put together for your own use – it is not shared with the meeting participants. Although it may be in a very rough format, it contains a detailed listing of the topics, key questions, and estimated timeframes for each topic. This working agenda will help you remember to cover the important points during the meeting.

But, suppose the meeting's topic has several subtopics. For example, imagine that you are scheduled to meet with a process owner to gain an understanding of the business objectives, major steps in the process, governance, key systems and applications, and regulatory environment. In this situation, you would be well advised to have an agenda listing these points. Frankly, there are just too many to remember. And, you should share this agenda with the process owner well in advance of the meeting's start, so this person can come prepared to discuss this wide array of topics.

Providing advance written agendas to the people with whom you are meeting has several benefits:

- If you are scheduled to meet with a person or people who have never been audited before, they may have preconceived or erroneous ideas about the audit process or the type of information you want to collect. Having the agenda in advance can quell concerns and nip them before they become obstacles or objections.

- When the people with whom you are meeting have the agenda in advance, they can set their expectations. And, they can prepare so that the topics can be covered quickly and efficiently. They may also realize that they need to invite additional people who can speak to the specific topics on your agenda. And, if no one on their team has the information you want to discuss, they can let you know, so you can figure out who you need to contact to get the information you need.
- Publishing the agenda enables the participants to read it. Although you may have described the meeting purpose in an email or during a telephone conversation, they may interpret the agenda differently once they see it in print. And, if they call you to discuss their perceived differences, all the better....you will be able to avoid a potential conflict and wasted time.

"Most things which are urgent are not important, and most things which are important are not urgent."

Dwight D. Eisenhower

6.5 Tips for Sequencing the Agenda Items

In case it's not obvious, I am a proponent of agendas – even if they are just the working ones that only you use. (Although it's better to share your agendas with the people with whom you will meet – it gives them a sense of control and keeps them from using the excuse: Had I known this is what you wanted to talk about I would have invited other people.....sent you the ABC report....told you I don't know a thing about this topic, etc.) Agendas, like lists, keep you organized and free up your mind to do other things during the meeting like listening to the participants' responses to your questions and thinking critically about the answers.

When preparing your agendas – including the working ones – urgent items are not the same as important ones. Urgent items are time sensitive; they require immediate attention. Because of this time sensitivity, these items create and warrant a reactive response.

Important items relate to one's mission or goal achievement, but might not require an immediate (i.e., urgent) response.

If you are not sure, you might want to emulate Dwight D. Eisenhower's decision model to help you prioritize tasks based on their urgency and determine the activities that are important and those that aren't.

	HIGH IMPORTANCE	LOW IMPORTANCE
High Urgency	Do it now.	Delegate it now.
Low Urgency	Plan it now.	Don't do it.

Keep the following points in mind because they will help you organize your ideas, achieve your meeting objective, and increase your meeting's efficiency:

- Put the less important issues at the top of the agenda, not the bottom. View them as quick hits that you can easily resolve. If you put them on the bottom, you may never get to them because you'll tend to spend all the time on the big issues.
- Schedule any urgent issues at the agenda's start because of their time sensitivity. Place nonurgent items down on the agenda – if you are going to miss any, you can more easily afford to miss these.
- Try to achieve a varied mix through the running order – if possible, avoid putting several heavy or controversial items together – vary the agenda to create changes in pace and intensity.
- Be aware of the tendency for people to be at their most sensitive at the beginning of meetings, especially if there are attendees who are eager to stamp their presence on proceedings. For this reason, it can be helpful to schedule a particularly controversial issue later in the sequence, which gives people a chance to settle down and relax first, and maybe get some of the sparring out of their systems over less significant items.
- Also be mindful of the lull that generally affects people after lunch, so try to avoid scheduling the most boring item of the agenda at this time if you have an early afternoon meeting; instead plan to get people participating and involved.

A couple of final thoughts about agendas:

- They are merely tools for structuring, ordering, and guiding the interview and preventing digressions and tangents. Don't spend hours creating them. If you are spending more time creating the agendas than actually speaking to the people responsible for the area under review, you are doing something wrong and wasting time.

- Acquire a reputation for having productive meetings. Here's how to do this: Before you publish the agenda, do the math when estimating time requirements. By that I mean:

  o Count up the topics (and subtopics) that you intend to discuss and then divide the number of topics – including the opening and the wrap up – into the total time allocated for the meeting. This will give you an average time per topic.

  o Then, consider the meeting's purpose (e.g., to collect information or to confirm information) to make sure you have scheduled enough time to do justice to the topic, (i.e., reach a viable decision or dispose of the agenda item in some other way so that it is addressed and doesn't become the proverbial gum on your shoe).

  o Then, think about whether any of the topics requires discussion. If a topic requires discussion, plan to add at least 20 minutes per topic, depending upon the severity and likelihood of the inherent risk and the complexity of the control design, gap, or operating error.

For example, if you wanted to talk about five different topics during a 60-minute meeting, each topic would need an average of 12 minutes. Now, imagine that three of the topics concern your preliminary observations or reactions to data provided by the constituent. And, just to make the situation clearer – imagine your preliminary observations and reactions consist of questions and conclusions related to control gaps over high inherent risks. In this situation, 12 minutes per topic will probably not be enough to get answers to your questions and discuss these three areas for the first time with your constituent.

- Remember to be flexible when using agendas during an interview. Depending on the situation, the topics may be addressed in a different order other than the way they are listed on the agenda. Don't get so hung up on your agenda that you cannot fully participate in the meeting as a facilitator.
- Set realistic expectations concerning the scope and depth of information to be covered during the meeting. When you receive tentative or noncommittal responses do not jump to conclusions that a control weakness exists. Keep in mind that each person you meet with will not know everything about the area or topic under discussion. Identify open issues in a matter-of-fact manner and address them after the meeting by speaking with other people.

Plan your work and work your plan.

Napoleon Hill
American self-help author

So far, we have focused on planning the meeting. Now let's concentrate on what you need to do to run it.

6.6 Tips for Running Effective Meetings

Following are some habits to get into if you want to garner the reputation for leading productive meetings:

Start and end on time… Unless of course the CEO (or other executive who is the centerpiece of your meeting) is running a few minutes late. When this happens, fill the wait time by addressing administrative topics (e.g., reminders to fill out time sheets). If the meeting is a routine one, like a status meeting, and the person who is supposed to address the first topic on the agenda is running late or experiencing connectivity issues, move onto the next topic on the agenda and forge ahead. You can always circle back to cover the first topic when the missing person shows up.

Start each meeting with a framework. A framework is a verbal statement expressed at the start describing:

- Your role and purpose. When you describe your role, consider adding a little background information to help the other person see you as a three-dimensional person – particularly if you are leading a virtual or telephone meeting. Let the other person know how long you have been with the company or in the department or working in the industry (if you are new to the company but experienced in the field).[1] Sharing this information about yourself encourages the person with whom you are meeting to share similar information.
- The meeting objectives – a description of what is to be accomplished by the end of the meeting and how this result relates to the rest of the audit or project.
- A summary of the agenda.
- The role of those in attendance (e.g., to comment, approve, work on the meeting topics).

You may be thinking why use a framework? The meeting purpose is stated in the agenda. While the agenda may be included in the meeting invitation, you have no assurance that the recipient read the purpose or, if it was read, it could have been misunderstood. Starting each of your meetings with a framework sets the tone and centers the attendees' attention on the purpose that needs to be achieved before the meeting's end.

If your meeting is actually an interview or a walk-through, frameworks clarify the participant's expectations of the meeting and forestall misunderstandings. Use of frameworks is one way to verify that you are interviewing the right people.

End each major topic and the meeting with a Wrap-up and Recap. You may want to "wrap up and recap" after each topic, particularly if the discussion was extended, highly detailed, complex, or technical. You can do this by:

- Summarizing what was discussed and decided.
- Providing the participants with feedback concerning how the meeting or interview went (e.g., the meeting purpose was accomplished, another meeting is needed, additional issues or potential problems were identified).

- Identifying open items.
- Stating the agreed upon steps to address the open items.
- Reiterating how the meeting results related to the rest of the audit (e.g., the audit is on schedule or delayed; the issues are similar to or different from those identified in the other areas under review).

At the end of the meeting, review your notes with the participants before you leave to confirm that they are accurate and relevant. Summarize the next steps in the audit or sprint, so that everyone knows what to expect, especially, if you may need to schedule another meeting.

Then, focus on increasing your ability to facilitate discussion: While prioritizing and organizing the meeting agenda is important, facilitating it effectively is just as important. Your ability to run the meeting – putting your plan into action – is critical. Facilitation is the process of enabling groups to work cooperatively and effectively. Literally, "to facilitate" means

WAYS TO BREAK THE ICE AND FUEL THE CONVERSATION

It's up to you to break the ice and not with the trite, "So, how are you doing?" Instead, you might comment on something on the person's wall or their choice in video backdrops. Whatever you decide to talk about, be sincere and interested.

Once the ice is broken, keep the talk moving by asking open-ended questions that require the other person to respond with more than a word or two. For example, if you opened the conversation by discussing the weekend's activities, don't just say, "How was your weekend?" Instead ask, "What was the best part of your weekend?" The latter is more engaging.

Some Topics to Avoid

- Stories of questionable taste – when in doubt, pick another topic
- Gossip
- Personal misfortunes
- How much things cost
- Controversial subjects if you don't know where everyone stands on them
- Health (yours or theirs)

Tips for Fueling a Conversation

- Be the first to say hello.
- Make an extra effort to remember and use the other person's name.
- Be able to succinctly tell others what you do.
- Be aware of open and closed body language – especially on video.
- Pose questions more often than making statements to get the other person's perspective.

"to make easier." It is particularly important in circumstances where people of diverse backgrounds, interests, and capabilities work together.

As a facilitator, your role is to:

- encourage participation,
- maintain focus on the task,
- help build small agreements among the team members,
- manage the group's process of decision-making, and
- enable a meeting or educational session to flow more smoothly.

Following are four important to-dos when you are the facilitator:

Create an open environment. Groups work best when individuals are made to feel comfortable expressing their ideas. Encourage all participants to listen to what others are saying. If a session is splintering into separate discussion groups, halt them politely and ask them to deal with one discussion at a time.

Involve all participants. In any group, some individuals will be less inclined to speak up. Watch out for signs that people are not involved. Be aware of any participant who is keeping their head down, doodling, or showing similar lack of engagement. Some people are more comfortable expressing their ideas in writing than saying them out loud. Encourage people to use the chat box to express their ideas during virtual meetings. (And, if you do this, get in the habit of pausing for several seconds to let people type their ideas.)

Some people may be so soft spoken that they are susceptible to interruptions by others. To engage and encourage these people, ask them for their opinions and comments. But before you do, say something like: I'd like to hear from someone who hasn't had the opportunity to share ideas yet. This way, you are giving these participants a heads-up that you would like them to contribute.

Another way to encourage quiet participants during virtual meetings is to send them a private chat message asking if they would like to weigh in on the topic. This private message lets them know that you are aware of who is contributing and that you would like their input.

Pay attention. As facilitator, you must be attentive to what is happening at all times. Do not get sidetracked into long discussions with individuals. Make sure that the meeting or interview stays on task and accomplishes its agenda.

Lead by example. You can encourage cooperative behavior by behaving in a way that is at all times honest, open, respectful, and nonpartisan. If a disagreement arises, do not take sides. Instead, remind the group of its goal or objectives and the criteria by which they will know they have achieved the desired results. Then, ask the group to resolve the issue. If the group gets bogged down or does not have the experience, knowledge, or authority to make the decision, escalate the issue after the meeting.

QUESTIONS TO FACILITATE DISCUSSION

FACT QUESTIONS:	What happened?
	Who did/said...?
	What are the steps?
REACTION QUESTIONS:	What is your reaction?
	Do you agree/disagree? Why?
	What is challenging about the process?
	What questions does this stimulate in your mind?
	What needs more clarification?
ANALYSIS QUESTIONS:	Why did they do...?
	What is the real source of conflict?
	Who seems to be most at fault?
APPLICATION QUESTIONS:	What are the implications for you in your job?
	How does it compare to your world?
	What can you use tomorrow at work?

6.7 But Be Ready to Intervene

Sometimes, despite your best efforts to plan and facilitate, things will happen and your meeting will begin to go off course. Interventions are techniques you can use to put things back on track when they have begun to go astray. Following are typical ways you can intervene and get involved:

- **Reinforce ground rules**. Keep people working with the process and ground rules that the group originally agreed to. "Remember, this is just the brainstorming stage; clarifications and discussion will follow later." Or "If you would like to speak, I need to see a raised hand, as we agreed. It doesn't work to have people cutting each other off."

- **Regain focus**. Use the goals, agenda, outcomes, activity at hand, or other ways to refocus the group. For example, "We're getting off track with this item. Remember our purpose is to decide on the rating; we can deal with the issue of report formatting, but we need to make a separate time for that." Or "Let's refocus; take a 5-minute break, then come back and let's get through this."

- **Accept and legitimize, then deal with or defer**. Accept participants' statements, even when emotional, without letting them take the group totally offtrack. For example, "It's clear that you have some very strong opinions about this. Let's keep thinking about how to turn these problems into solutions." "Wow, that's an important point. Perhaps we should take 5 minutes to address that point before moving on. Does everyone agree?" "That's a critical issue. Keep it in mind because we're going to talk about this a few items down our agenda."

- **Use humor**. Or someone else's humor. Allow for some laughter and good-natured joking. It can help to diffuse tension and lighten difficult situations.

- **Ask or say "what's going on?"** Being direct can be a useful technique when there is clear tension or resistance. Be prepared to deal with the answer.

- **Boomerang**. When someone at the meeting attempts to question the process or otherwise wants to take the group in a different direction, it can be helpful to turn that question to the group. You can ask, "Well, what do you think?" or "Let's consider that question for a minute. What are other people's thoughts?" or "What does the group think?" This technique works very well when the other meeting participants are peers or outrank the person who is questioning the approach. If the person who wants to question the process outranks most of the people in the room, then you need to reinforce the ground rules, especially when this guidance was approved by a governance group or executive.

- **Break**. Call a break if participants look like their attention is waning. Have a stretch. Take frequent breaks when meeting virtually to keep attendees focused and stimulated. But....

do not take a break if the conversation is becoming crucial or conflicted. Doing so will just solidify the discord. Refer to Chapter 10 Managing and resolving conflict for ways to deal with disagreements and potential conflict.

6.8 Notes

In our profession, notes are important. We need to be able to support our results and conclusions. Consequently, I would be remiss in ending this chapter without discussing when and how to take notes without derailing your meeting.

One of the benefits of virtual meetings is the record button. It's a wonderful invention – as long as all parties know that it is on and how the recorded session's data will be used. Press the record button and you are freed up to take notes – real notes, not a stenographic transcription of the conversation. Best of all, you can play it back as many times as you need to understand how the process or control works.

If you are meeting virtually or in person, maintain eye contact with the others in attendance, particularly the person who is answering your question. Do not allow your note taking to become an obstruction to the exchange of information. And, if you are meeting virtually, and think that you can enter your notes online because no one can see you – remember that the sound of typing is annoying to other participants.

If your meetings are mostly teleconferences and no one can see you, the primary thing you have to remember is *no one can see you*. So… when you are silently transcribing every word the person on the other end of the phone just told you, silence fills the line. That unexplained, protracted silence that follows the person's answer to your question can be painful – not for you because you are busy writing, but for the other people who are participating in the meeting.

If the person who just answered your question has to watch or listen as you fill your notepad with a lengthy explanation, this individual will become nervous, defensive, impatient, or hostile (depending on the length of the meeting). At a minimum, don't be surprised if this person starts to give you shorter answers, if only to reduce the time spent watching or listening to you write. Of course, you could avoid this problem by replacing transcription with note-taking.

6.8.1 Tips for Effective Note-taking

- Listen to the other person's responses before you make notes. If you are writing as this person is speaking you are NOT listening.
- Make your notes after you restate your understanding of what the person has said *and this person agrees that your understanding is correct.* Why write something down and then confirm its accuracy only to find out you misunderstood what was said?

  The important time to take notes is after the other person tells you that your understanding is correct. And, making a note at this point will actually reinforce your understanding and make it easier to remember what the other person tells you. Why? Because you will have expressed your understanding in two ways: first, your verbal confirmation, which should be expressed in your own words and not a parroting of what you heard. Second, your written record of this understanding.

- Write just the facts. Refrain from writing opinions, perspectives, and irrelevant remarks. Do not try to write every word that is spoken.
- Do not write long sentences of explanation unless absolutely necessary (i.e., a specific formula, equation, or URL. Instead, choose brief and concise words).

If more than one auditor is involved in an interview, one should listen and the other should take notes. This enables the auditor who is speaking or leading an interview to maintain the conversational flow while the other concentrates on documenting the responses. During the wrap-up after each topic or at the end of the meeting, the two auditors should switch roles. The auditor who was taking the notes should verbally summarize them and get verbal confirmation from the respondents that the data is accurate. While this is happening, the other auditor who was formerly leading the meeting should now take the notes. This switch in roles keeps the meeting moving along.

6.8.2 Special Tips for Telephone and Virtual Meetings

- Do not take the call on speakerphone because it will make it harder for the other person to hear you. If you must use a speakerphone because several people from your team and the participant's team are on the line, ask each person to identify himself or herself before speaking (e.g., This is Muffy and I have a question).

- As you answer the phone, smile, identify yourself, and speak clearly. Do not chew gum while on the phone.
- At the start of the conversation, state your objectives. Verify that the participant's understanding of the conversation is the same or similar to yours.
- Speak slowly and confidently. Keep your questions clear and succinct. Don't ramble. You want to portray yourself as an organized professional and a good listener.
- Pause more frequently and for a slightly longer duration than you would during an in-person meeting or video conference to give the other person more "think" time because they don't have the visual cues that occur during in-person meetings.
- Restate more frequently than you would in an in-person meeting to verify that the participant agrees with your understanding of the discussion.
- Try not to interrupt the participants as they are talking – unless you're certain they are on a tangent.
- Keep the interview on track. Stay focused on the key points. If the participant is rambling off-topic, find a way to bring the conversation back or let the person know you understand and move on to the next question.
- Make it conversational by asking the right follow-up questions and insert short snippets here and there (i.e., "Sounds like a difficult situation. How did you deal with that?") to make the participant feel more comfortable with you, which contributes to an open and honest dialogue.
- Listen and focus your full attention on the interview; don't multitask. Make sure your cell phone is muted and your email notification is disabled.
- Fill the silence you create by letting the other person know what you're doing (e.g., thinking, making a note, locating information).

For Skill Practice

1. Think about the last three meetings you organized. What were the goals for each meeting? Was each goal accomplished within the established timeframe? Did each meeting have an agenda? In what ways could you improve the meeting's effectiveness? To what extent could you run a meeting for a similar purpose (e.g., project kickoff, status meeting) more efficiently?

2. Think about those who participated in the last three group meetings you facilitated. To what extent did everyone participate and exchange ideas? What techniques did you use to get everyone to contribute and exchange ideas? If these techniques did not work, what other approaches can you use if you are in a similar situation in the future (i.e., what will be your Plan B?).

Chapter Summary

- Before scheduling a meeting, determine whether you need one at all. What information do you need? Is it background or historic information that you can get through research and reading? Or, do you need to collaborate with another person? Do you need the answer to a simple question or an uncomplicated situation? If so, send an email to the person who can answer your question and no meeting is necessary.
- The benchmarks of an effective agenda are that they will help you organize your ideas, achieve your meeting objective, and increase your meeting's efficiency.
- An effective meeting facilitator creates an open environment, involves all participants, pays attention, and leads by example.

Note

1 If you are a new college hire, stating that you have no experience is not advised because this statement will do nothing to inspire confidence in the person with whom you are meeting. Instead, let them know that you are a new college hire (they'll be able to figure this out on their own, so you may as well lead with it) and then mention something about your studies that indicates your interest in the industry, field, or role. For example, if you are assigned to a Treasury audit, mention that you were a Finance major.

My Takeaway Game Plan

My Goal is:

Behaviors I will *start* to achieve my goal...

Behaviors I will *continue* to achieve my goal...

Behaviors I will *stop* to achieve my goal...

Leading and Lagging Indicators – How I'll Measure My Results

7

SPEAKING WITH TACT, CONFIDENCE, AND IMPACT

All speaking is public speaking whether it's to one person or a thousand.

Roger Love
American vocal coach

I deliberately decided not to entitle this chapter "Presentation Skills." The word "presentation" conjures up images of speeches, monologues, and other one-directional communications during which the speaker either:

- clasps a podium with white knuckles,
- stands swaying in a barrier-free environment, or
- drones on during a webinar while delivering remarks that were either memorized or read verbatim on innumerable PowerPoint slides.

What's your reaction when asked to speak? Are you thrilled, excited, eager? Or, would you rather have a root canal with no pain medicine? Whenever I lead presentation skills training sessions, I am constantly amazed by the number of people who would prefer to be anywhere other than this class. The thought of having to speak in front of a group causes them to panic and freeze up. Yet you can't complete your work without talking to someone: your boss, your team, the process, risk, or control owner. Every time you speak during a meeting, you are making a presentation. It may be a formal one; it may be extemporized comments in response to someone's unplanned question. Either way, your response is a presentation. So, I suggest reframing how you think about presentations and view them as an ordinary part of your work. And, since you will need to communicate with various people many times a day, the ability to communicate with tact, confidence, and impact is a core competency – one that will set you apart from others with similar technical backgrounds.

> The best way to sound like you know what you're talking about is to know what you're talking about.
>
> **Anonymous**

If you plan to remember only one thing from this book, make it this quote. Promise yourself that you will only speak about the subjects you know whether you are delivering prepared remarks at a formal meeting or responding to an impromptu question during a daily huddle. This idea is a cousin to the concept of always telling the truth because the truth is easier to remember than a lie.

If you speak only about what you know, you will:

INCREASE:	REDUCE:
• Your self-confidence.	• Your presentation preparation time.
• Your ability to focus on the needs of those listening to you.	• Any natural nervousness.
• Your natural ability to use different words to deliver your message so that the listeners understand.	• The need to check your notes while you deliver your message.

7.1 Getting Rid of the Nerves

Each time I start a training session on presentation skills, I ask the attendees what they would like to accomplish as a result of participating in the program. Without fail, several people want to learn how to deliver their message without being nervous at all. This just isn't possible. Nervousness is a part of the process. It's part of that flight or fight response as your body begins to increase its adrenaline as it gears up and gets ready to communicate. So, the goal isn't how to get rid of the nervousness (because you won't be able to as long as you are alive). The goal is really how to manage the natural body response to situations in which you need to deliver your message to others.

As a conference presenter and trainer, I speak to thousands each year. And, each time, as I look at the audience and get ready to make my opening remarks, I feel the twinge of nervousness. I know. You'd think I'd be over it by now, but that sense of excitement gives me the energy to start my presentation. The nervousness is a natural physical response. How you manage it makes all the difference. I use the following exercises to counteract potential negative anxiety and focus it to direct the energy and deliver my message.

7.1.1 Breathing Exercises

In order to project your voice so that others can hear you, you need to breathe naturally. Unfortunately, stress causes you to breathe shallowly. Shallow breathing makes it difficult to project your voice. It will also cause you to run out of air before you finish your sentence – which also makes it difficult for others to hear you.

Practice your breathing by using the following two exercises:

- Exhale.
- Inhale slowly while counting to five.
- Exhale slowly while counting to five.

Repeat this exercise several times until your breathing becomes steady and even. Begin this exercise the moment you feel the first twinge of nervousness. It will help you focus your energy and remain calm.

Another exercise that will help you regulate your breathing and manage your nervousness is to:

1. Exhale.
2. Inhale, until you cannot inhale anymore air.
3. Exhale, slowly while counting out loud.

Repeat this exercise several times. Each time you should look to count to a higher number as a way of increasing your breathing capacity. Do not speed up your counting in order to reach a higher number. If you are in a communal space count silently to yourself.

The purpose of these exercises is to increase the amount of air you inhale and to increase air support when you speak. The key to both of these exercises is keeping your shoulders from moving up as you inhale. Quite often, when we take deep breaths, we tend to pick up and drop our shoulders as we inhale and exhale. Raising your shoulders actually forces you to take shorter breaths. When you inhale, place your hand directly below your stomach. You should feel the air first filling your diaphragm and then your chest. If you raise your shoulders when you inhale, you are only filling your chest cavity with air. The great thing about these exercises is that you can do them anywhere. And....no one will realize that you are doing them.

7.1.2 Mental Rehearsal

The power of mental rehearsal is defined by the expression, "What the mind can conceive, the body can achieve." Mental rehearsal is equivalent to a dress rehearsal in your mind. Prior to the opening of a play, the actors memorize and rehearse their lines. During the dress rehearsal, they perform the entire play exactly as they would if an audience were watching.

Prior to delivering your presentation, you should perform your own "dress rehearsal" in your mind. The evening before your presentation, find a quiet place and lie down. In your mind's eye, see yourself delivering your presentation. Imagine yourself watching the audience members' expressions as they respond beautifully and accurately to your presentation. If you do not like your response to a question from your imaginary audience, try again to answer the question. Continue to mentally rehearse your answers until you are satisfied. Once satisfied, commit your responses to memory.

Mental rehearsal is probably the most powerful exercise you can do to prepare to deliver your message because you are consciously seeing yourself succeed in your mind's eye. This exercise is especially helpful if you engage in it right before nodding off to sleep the night before you need to deliver your message, so that the images of your successful delivery are etched in your mind.

7.1.3 Vocal Rehearsal

Practice vocalizing your presentation, especially if you do not attend many meetings or the message you need to deliver is very important. Vocal rehearsals enable you to **hear** how you sound (i.e., whether you talk too fast or slowly) when delivering your presentation. It also enables you to quickly identify those overly long and complicated sentences that read well but sound terrible. After you vocalize your message, you may find what you want to:

- Fine-tune your word choice. (Did you stumble over any word?)
- Rework your segues. (Did each transition clearly set up the next topic?)
- Change your intonations. (Does your voice convey excitement and variety?)
- Remove "audible pauses." (Do you hear yourself say "uhs," "you know," "you see"?)
- Slow your speech down so that you can enunciate clearly and pronounce the words correctly.

Get in the habit of pausing and breathing when you finish a statement. This will immediately reduce your audible pauses. Remember that the other people at the meeting are listening to your message and processing it in a lag. By pausing to breathe when you reach a period, you are giving your audience some time to think about your message. They may have some questions and your pause will give them time to pose them. This is especially important when delivering your message virtually. Your listeners not only need mental processing time, they need time to find the chat box or unmute button so they can pose their questions and make their comments.

7.1.4 Physical Rehearsal

Experienced presenters know that they must be mindful of their body posture – even when presenting virtually. When you rehearse, take the time to focus on the impact of your body language and eye contact:

- Are you standing in the front of the room or in a place that provides the attendees with an unobstructed view of you?
- Are you seated? If you are sitting, be sure you are not swaying or swiveling as you deliver your message. If you have the unconscious tendency to swivel – particularly when you are stressed – you might want to sit on a straight-backed chair that does not move.
- Do you walk around the room or do you stand in one place? While you can move from one spot to another as you deliver your message, you do not want to pace while speaking because the attendees will be distracted by the constant motion. If you

find yourself standing in one place during a group-live meeting, make notations in your "script" to identify times when you could move to a different spot.

When presenting virtually, consider where the camera is relative to where you are sitting. If you are using the camera in your laptop, keep in mind that the other person will see your face from the neck up. So, if you are using your hands, the other person will not see these gestures unless you bring your hands near your face. Alternatively, you may want to back away about 2 feet away from your screen to create a broader viewing angle for the virtual meeting attendees. Also, be sure to look directly into the camera when speaking, so that the other person views you as making eye contact.

Be sure to test all equipment prior to the presentation on the device you will use during the meeting and confirm the audience size and room layout if you are presenting in a group-live format. When presenting virtually, be sure to test all of the features you intend to use: file sharing, whiteboards, file uploads, chat, and polling.

7.1.5 Identifying "Friendly Faces"

Just before you begin your presentation, make a mental note of those audience members who appear to be the most interested or empathetic. Ideally, you want to identify a "friendly face" in each corner of the room (or screen) so that during your presentation you can shift your gaze from one "friendly face" to another, giving the appearance of looking at everyone in the room.

When presenting virtually, use the gallery view so that you can view all of the photos periodically during the meeting as a break from looking directly into the camera.

Great is the art of beginning, but greater is the art of ending.

Henry Wadsworth Longfellow

American poet

7.2 Planning Your Message

Whenever you need to communicate your ideas, answer the following questions and you'll find that your message practically develops itself.

First, what's your objective? Typical objectives are to entertain, persuade, motivate an audience or obtain, clarify, or give information.

Another way to think about your goal is to begin with the end in mind. Imagine that you have just finished delivering your message. How will whoever listens to you be different afterward? What will they know or be able to do that they couldn't before they listened to your message? For example, let's imagine that your goal is to get others in your organization to involve risk management, information security, and audit professionals at the very start of business projects and initiatives instead of waiting until the end. As you consider your objective also consider whether your presentation is really necessary and will add value. Consider what would happen if you said nothing.

The second question you need to answer is who is your audience, so that you can come up with the WIIFM. This acronym represents the thought that is in everyone's mind whenever they listen to someone else speak: What's In It For Me? Each listener is trying to figure out as quickly as possible whether you have something to say that is going to benefit them. The earlier in your message you let the listener know the benefit, the better. And, the more the benefit is something very important to your listener, the better.

So, you need to be able to imagine the profile of who will be listening as clearly as possible. What do they already know about your message? Are they already proponents of your message or are they opposed or resistant to it? Will your message be something they never heard or considered before? The profile of your audience will affect the details you include and wording you use. If the audience is already a proponent of your ideas, you can spend more time on other aspects of the message. If the audience is hearing your idea for the first time, you may want to spend some time providing context so that everyone understands why your message is important.

Imagine that you need to share your message in the prior example with the Board of Directors (or the Risk or Audit Committee). The WIIFM you describe to them may be early warning and ability to avert problems and waste (problem avoidance – the stick). Or, you might tout increased organizational ability to meet deadlines while simultaneously delivering competitive solutions. Now, imagine that you have the same objective but you are speaking directly to those who head up the business areas that you want to persuade to involve risk management, information security, and audit professionals earlier. The perspective of this group is not going to be the same as that of the Board. This group may believe that your request is going to mean more work for them. Some may wonder why risk management, information security, and audit professionals need to get involved earlier and they might think that this involvement is a waste of time or will cause delays to the project or initiative. Consequently, when you share your message with this group, the benefits that you describe may be different or, if they are similar, the wording may be different.

Once you have the answers to the questions concerning your objective and the audience, you are ready to address the tactical questions so that you can develop your message:

- Where will I be speaking (i.e., in front of the group or from a seated position in a virtual setting)?
- Will I need any visual aids or handouts to make my point more easily understood?
- How much time do I have to make my point?
- Am I the only speaker or one of many?
- If others will also be speaking, at what time in the agenda am I scheduled to speak?

WHAT TO DO TO GET ORGANIZED WITH LITTLE OR NO NOTICE:
Set and address the objective of your presentation.
Speak about a topic you know.
Remember and address the audience needs.
Select a presentation strategy.
Keep your sentences short and simple.

7.3 Strategies for Organizing Presentations

Your goals define the overall desired results of your presentation. Is it to entertain, persuade, motivate an audience and/or obtain, clarify, or give information? Objectives are critical because they show the audience the exact purpose of the presentation and allow you to measure your presentation's results against a specific standard.

The following are some strategies (or formats) for organizing your message. Each one's effectiveness depends on:

- Your objective.
- The audience needs and expectations.
- The situation.

7.3.1 STRATEGY 1. The Critical Linkage[TM1]

Describe the process or business objectives and the major steps in the process that are in project or audit scope or just the one(s) that will be addressed during your presentation.

Describe the inherent risk (i.e., what could go wrong to threaten the achievement of the process or business objective or the function that your presentation addresses), its trigger or cause, and its consequence to the business overall.

Describe the control that addresses the inherent risk or the control gap, design flaw, or execution error.

Describe the corrective action needed to address the root cause of the control gap, design flaw, or execution error.

7.3.2 STRATEGY 2. The Attention Grabber

- Get the audience's attention.
- Describe the audience's need.
- Satisfy this need.
- Have the audience visualize their need satisfied.
- Ask the audience to take action.

7.3.3 STRATEGY 3. The Rational Approach

- Describe a situation or an example.
- Make your point.
- Explain the reason or rationale for your point.

7.3.4 STRATEGY 4. The Devil's Advocate

- Make your point.
- Deliver a counterpoint or devil's advocacy position.

- Describe the argument.
- Draw conclusions.

7.3.5 STRATEGY 5. *The Chronological Approach*

- Determine if the background of a situation is essential to dealing with the current condition.
- Organize your notes based on a timeline (i.e., from start to end or from current state to the precipitating event).
- Begin with the first action taken and proceed to each subsequent action in the order in which they occurred.

7.3.6 STRATEGY 6. *Tell 'Em, Tell 'Em, and Tell 'Em Again Approach*

This strategy is the easiest for audiences to follow.

- Begin by stating the purpose or goal of the presentation's topic. Essentially, you are telling the audience what will be covered.
- Next, cover the topic in sufficient detail based on your audience's needs. Effectively, you are telling them the message.
- Finally, summarize what you have told them.

Regardless of the strategy you select, allow time to practice so that you can deliver your message with confidence. During your practice sessions, be sure to Time your presentation. Exceeding your time allocation communicates to your audience that you are unprepared.

7.4 Analogies and Metaphors – An Easier Way to Talk Techie

If you have to talk about something very technical, you may find it helpful to use an analogy or metaphor. Analogies are a partial likeness between two things that are compared (e.g., the Internet and a superhighway). Metaphors are words or phrases that apply to an idea in a figurative, as opposed to literal way (e.g., "the evening of one's life.") By using analogies and metaphors you can relate technical ideas to things the audience may be more familiar with in their own lifestyles, environments, or skills.

The more complex your subject matter, the more analogies you will probably require to communicate it.

Plan several analogies, stories, and metaphors that are customized for the audience for each point. By thinking ahead about how you might explain concepts, you'll have the special examples you need. Even if you decide to use perfectly good tried-and-true standbys (e.g., "Think of the Internet as a highway"), put life and color into them. No matter how perfect an analogy is, the audience won't be energized unless you are.

The following table provides some basic formulas for creating analogies. In the examples, the letter "X" represents a technical topic, while a blank space represents your analogy:

ANALOGY TYPE	FORMULA
Thing-to-Thing	In this formula, a technical "thing," such as an instrument, tool, technology, or product, is compared to something else. Example: "X" is like a _____, in that it shares the following attributes: (list attributes). "X" is to its environment as _____ is to its environment (explain similar relationships the two things have with respect to their environments). "X" can be dismantled into components "A," "B," and "C," much in the same way that _____ can be dismantled into components "D," "E," and "F." (Here you compare the similarities between what two things are composed of – ingredients, structure, anatomy, etc.). The history of "X" and its development is very similar to the history of _____ and its development. "X's" product life cycle is much like _____'s product life cycle.
Process-to-Process	In this formula, a technical process is compared to another process, whether it occurs in people, nature, civilization, or another technology: "X" functions just like _____ (describe physical attributes of movement: mechanics, speed, gracefulness, direction or rotation, etc.). In order to complete its task, "X" goes through the same stages as _____. The process of "X" is much like the process of _____, in that both perform the same types of functions.

ANALOGY TYPE	FORMULA
Symbol-to-Symbol	In this formula, the particular qualities (in terms of what they mean to us and how they affect us) of a technical thing or process is compared to the corresponding qualities of another thing or process: "X" means the same thing to us as _____. Both are vital to us in the same way. "X" represents (choose a quality, such as freedom, empowerment, efficiency) to us just as _____ does. We can identify ourselves with "X" much in the same way that we can identify with _____.
Person-to-Person	In this formula, an individual from the technical field is compared to an individual from an unrelated field. The two are compared for the significance of their contribution, their personal attributes, or their method for going about achieving something: "X" is to her field just as _____ is to his field. "X," "Y," and "Z" work as a team, just like _____, _____, and _____ work as a team. "X" was known as the _____ of his field, much like _____ was known as the _____ to his field. "X" found success the same way as _____ found success. "X" was like _____. Both had the following attributes (e.g., ambition, confidence, out of the box thinking, etc.).
Circumstance-to-Circumstance	In this formula, a circumstance (not a thing or process, but rather the conditions that fostered its qualities or its limitations) is compared to another circumstance with similar things or processes that are inherent to it. Technology "X" was required for a specific set of circumstances in the same way that the technology _____ was required for its own circumstances. The problem of "X" is similar to the problem of _____. Both require _____ for a solution.

Techniques for Developing and Maintaining Audience Involvement

Following are some things to keep in mind when you deliver your message either virtually or in person:

1 Keep a relaxed, upbeat facial expression.
2 If the meeting is virtual, look into the camera, not the faces on the screen.
3 Once you've planned your message, you have to deliver. Keep the expression "make your plan and then work with your plan" in mind. Be sure to follow the presentation as planned. When

you are expected to deliver a formal presentation (e.g., at a Board meeting), improvisation is risky and should be avoided.

4 If you are standing, be sure to keep hands out of pockets (because on camera it will look like you are slump shouldered. Make sure your weight is evenly distributed and your feet are a shoulder's width apart if you are at a raised desk or presenting barrier-free in front of a room.

5 If you will be seated, sit in your chair without rocking, swiveling, or swaying.

6 Place both feet on the ground when speaking from a seated position so that your shoulders appear even and level.

7 Sit upright in your chair, so that your back is straight and not touching the chair back. Occupy the first third of the chair (i.e., lean in slightly) to convey energy and interest to others.

8 Keep arms uncrossed so that you appear open-minded in group-live and virtual settings. Allow your arms and legs to move naturally if you are standing.

9 Use natural hand gestures that complement and underscore your message – but don't point a finger at the audience.

10 Keep hands away from your face (i.e., eyes, nose, and mouth). You want to appear open to seeing everyone and talking openly.

As you deliver your message, you want to establish an environment that projects your credibility and competency, encourages participation, fosters an open exchange of ideas and experiences, and sets a positive attitude or tone. To do this, begin by reconsidering each use of jargon and acronym. Are the technical terms really necessary? Can you find ordinary words to convey your message? Whenever possible, eliminate the use of highly specialized auditing, accounting, or other technical language. Expressions like "properly accounted for" and "inappropriate transactions" don't mean much to people without an accounting or audit background. Get in the habit of speaking plainly: Say what you mean and mean what you say.

If you cannot avoid using technical terminology, provide a written glossary of all terms in a handout and explain any jargon you decide to include. If you intend to use specialized technical language, be prepared to explain it without using more jargon.

Avoid filler comments like: "It's obvious...," "As you all know...,", "It's common knowledge that..." These are condescending and add no value to your remarks. You were asked to speak because you are the expert and someone thought you could pass along some of that expertise. And, if what you're saying really is obvious, why bother to mention it at all?

By taking the following actions, you can build rapport with the audience and increase your credibility in their minds:

- Look at them (or directly at the camera during virtual sessions) and rephrase their questions before responding.
- Establish credibility as an experienced professional by mentioning the aspects of your background that are most pertinent to the presentation's topic and objectives.
- Create a need: make sure that the audience understands how they will benefit from the presentation.
- Use personal war stories to either introduce material or underscore key points. Tell no more than 1–2 stories for each key point. Make sure that war stories are indicative of general trends, not special or obscure cases.
- Develop a sense of personal responsibility for the audience. Talk in terms of their expectations, needs, goals, etc.
- Use the Critical Linkage™ to frame and deliver messages relating to discussions concerning inherent risks and controls. This model will align the interests of the process, risk, or control owner with yours.
- Give periodic summaries of your key points, particularly if your presentation is long.

7.5 Handling Audience Questions

At the start of your delivery, if you have a short amount of time to speak, you may want to let the audience know that you will allow time for questions at the end once you have finished. This way you can convey your message (which may answer some or all of their questions) without dilution and without running the risk that a question may create a tangent and waste time.

If you are delivering a longer presentation or an internal training session, you should let the audience members know that you would like them to stop you when they have a question. This way, if there are any misunderstandings about your message, they are resolved earlier rather than later. And, in the event that a couple of the questions are off base, you still have enough time to make your points.

Following are some ways to handle questions like a pro:

- Restate the questions questions before answering them. This way, everyone hears and understands the question before you respond. More importantly, it gives you the opportunity to make sure that you understand the question and its intent before you respond. You don't want to answer a question that wasn't asked.
- Listen to your audience. Do not interrupt them as they formulate questions or respond to questions you have posed. During virtual meetings, wait at least 10–15 seconds before closing poll questions or discussing responses attendees may have entered into the chat function.
- Make sure that audience members listen to each other. Allow only one person to speak at a time and discourage side conversations. During virtual meetings, ask everyone to mute their mikes unless they have a question or comment.
- Treat all audience members as valued contributors to the discussion. Don't play favorites. Avoid saying, "That was an excellent suggestion" or "Great question" because these subjective comments imply that not all audience questions are excellent. If you want to recognize the person who made the comment or asked the question, you can say: "Thank you for bringing up that point."
- When you don't know the answer, note the audience member's name and promise to follow-up later with a response.
- Show enthusiasm by smiling and by making and maintaining eye contact with the audience (which means looking into the camera during virtual meetings).

For Skill Practice

1. Think about the things you are asked to discuss at various meetings. In what ways could you use analogies or metaphors to make your message more relevant to your listeners?

2. Review the notes from your last three presentations. How many technical terms did you use? What ordinary expressions or analogies could you have used instead?

3. Many people do not understand the difference between inherent and residual risk. How can you explain these important concepts using plain language?

4. Think about the last three times you have had to speak to a group during a meeting:

   • Did you accomplish your objective?
   • How did you organize your message (e.g., using the Critical Linkage™, beginning with an attention grabber or tell 'em)?
   • Was your ending as strong as your start?

Chapter Summary

• Speak only about the subject you know whether you are delivering prepared remarks at a formal meeting or when responding to an impromptu question during a daily huddle or meeting.

• Nervousness is part of the process of delivering a message. The goal isn't to get rid of it; it's to manage the natural body responses when you need to deliver your message to others. To deal with it, practice breathing exercises; rehearse mentally, vocally, and physically; and identify the friendly faces in your audience.

Note

1 This is a COSO-based mental model I devised after working with thousands of auditors and risk managers. It's a practical way to think about and approach risk-based auditing. You'll find a more in-depth discussion in my book, *Mastering the Five Tiers of Audit Competency: The Essence of Effective Auditing*.

My Takeaway Game Plan

My Goal is:

Behaviors I will *start* to achieve my goal...

Behaviors I will *continue* to achieve my goal...

Behaviors I will *stop* to achieve my goal...

Leading and Lagging Indicators – How I'll Measure My Results

8

DELIVERING BAD NEWS WITHOUT CAUSING BAD FEELINGS

In the middle of difficulty lies opportunity.

Albert Einstein

8.1 Bad News – A Matter of Perception

Let's start by recognizing bad news in audit and risk management for what it is: something the other person doesn't want to hear. It may be something we think the other person will argue or disagree with, like knowing that we consider the function they manage to be a high-risk one.

At some point or another, you will have to deliver a message that others will not want to hear. While you might not view this news as negative, your opinion isn't the one that determines how the message is perceived and received. Perception, as always, is defined by the person or people who receive it.

Depending on the situation, you will have to communicate that inherent risks in some processes are high, controls thought to be in place aren't, or controls are not working as intended. Or, you may have to tell the Audit Committee Chair that several audits or advisory projects are delayed. You get the idea….the person who has to receive and deal with your message will not be happy.

When you are in these situations, keep a couple of things in mind. First, forgive yourself for being the bearer of bad news. You are not causing the distress…the news is. And, you didn't create the news, you just need to report it factually. Your message may be a confirmation of something the other person already knows.

That said, your message can still evoke an emotional response from the person who receives it. Consequently, your ability to deliver bad news calls for tact, diplomacy, and concern for the well-being of both you and the other person. At the same time, you need to make sure that your communications are timely. Fight the tendency to procrastinate delivering news you know will make others unhappy until you find the perfect time and place. Perfect times and places don't exist.

> Bad news isn't wine; it doesn't improve with age.
>
> **Colin Powell**

8.2 Sooner Is Better than Later

You need to communicate your results, including any bad news, as soon as possible if you want to have surprise-free audits and advisory projects. Do not wait to communicate until the closing conference. Get in the habit of discussing issues as they come up. If you do this, you will find that you are discussing situations when they are small and manageable – so small and manageable that what you discuss doesn't come across as bad news at all.

When you communicate your observations and results to the process, risk, or control owners as they occur, you may find out that your information is incomplete or that you have misinterpreted the data you received. Consider the following example.

Muffy, the auditor, has just finished testing a monitoring control that is supposed to detect errors in refund payments. Muffy's test results indicate that nearly all of the items she examined were not handled correctly. But before concluding that the monitoring control is not working as intended, Muffy decides to touch base with Izzy, the business manager, responsible for the control's performance. During this impromptu conversation, Muffy finds out that she selected the test items from the wrong database, which causes her to realize that a control execution error may not really exist. She heads off to test the monitoring control again using transactions from the right database and finds out that the control is working as intended. This quick check-in conversation has averted a misunderstanding.

Having a series of status conversations like this enables you to double-check your understanding of the area, its inherent risks, control design, and operating effectiveness, and will save you time in the long run. Imagine if Muffy had waited to have the conversation with Izzy until closer to the exit conference or during the closing meeting itself. Instead of getting ready to wrap up the audit, she may have needed to perform some additional testing. At the very least, she would have spent time writing up an issue that really wasn't one.

In the example, Muffy thought she had identified a control execution error, but didn't. But, what if your understanding of the control design was on target and the execution error existed. The sooner you communicate control gaps, design flaws, or execution errors, and anything you know about the root cause of these situations, the sooner business management can take corrective action. In some cases, management could make improvements before the audit is over. And, if this remediation works as intended, you will have contributed to improved organizational results.

Luck favors the prepared mind.

Louis Pasteur

8.3 Planning the Message

We've already established that you didn't create the bad news that you need to report. That's true, but you can control and are responsible for how you communicate the message. Consequently, you need to think carefully about the words you will use and how you will organize your thoughts.

1. Prepare for the conversation by using the Critical Linkage™ as the framework for your message. This model will enable you to communicate risk-based reasons for your message.

   - Start your message with a brief description of the process or functional objective under review (e.g., we are auditing commission calculation to make sure that our sales people are receiving the correct amount of commission for the sales they have made).
   - Then, summarize the inherent risk (e.g., one of the inherent risks we're focused on is making sure that sales people do not receive duplicate payments).

- Then discuss the condition of controls over this risk based on the interviews and testing you have completed (e.g., a control gap exists, a control design flaw exists, or a control execution error exists).

Critical Linkage™ from Mastering the Five Tiers of Audit Competency.

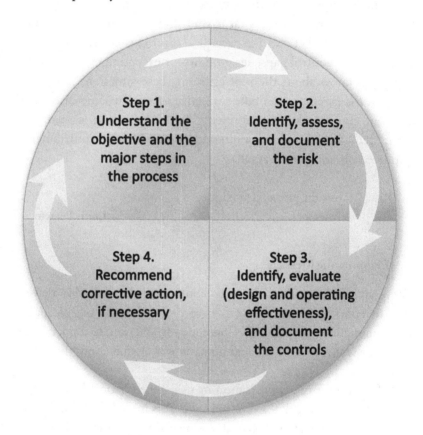

Step 1.
Understand the objective and the major steps in the process

Step 2.
Identify, assess, and document the risk

Step 4.
Recommend corrective action, if necessary

Step 3.
Identify, evaluate (design and operating effectiveness), and document the controls

2. Think about what you will say and what you won't say. Sometimes background details help; other times they confuse and complicate the message. Consider what your audience already knows about the situation and their predisposition toward the situation. Use this information to determine the amount and nature of the details you need to provide. For example, if you are speaking to a process, risk, or control owner who is very familiar with the situation, providing background information is unnecessary.

Typically, an executive audience wants to know:

- What's wrong?
- How or why did it happen?
- How bad is it?
- How and when will it be fixed?

When describing how bad the situation is, make sure that your response is consistent with the entity or area's overall risk rating. For example, if the overall entity or area's inherent risk rating is moderate or medium, it would be illogical for any issue identified during testing to be rated critical or high.

3. Keep the audience in mind. Who will be on the receiving end of your message? Will you deliver the bad news to an executive or a process owner or a team lead that owns or performs the control (i.e., someone who is doing the work as an analyst, underwriter, or department member). Identifying your audience will help you determine how much detail to include in your message. It will also help you determine the words to use to convey the facts. If the audience is executive in nature, use ordinary business language and minimize the technical terminology and references to templates, forms, and fields.

4. Analyze your findings to gain insight regarding the risk management culture. To do this, you might want to refer to the *Internal Control Maturity Model*.[1] If you have determined that no policies or standards exist (i.e., what good looks like is undefined), this indicates an immature risk management culture, one in which business managers and leaders believe that risk management is the auditors' or risk managers' responsibility. When discussing issues with someone who works in this environment, spend time discussing this person's responsibility for business results, including addressing the vulnerabilities and risks that could lead to negative or undesired outcomes.

At the next level of increased risk management cultural maturity, policies exist but the controls are not adequately designed (i.e., one or two attributes may be missing like consistent evidence that the control was performed). At the third level of risk management cultural maturity, policies exist, controls are well-designed, but they are not operating consistently or effectively (i.e., there's a gap between what's supposed to be happening as described in the policy or guidance and what is actually occurring). As an organization's risk management culture matures to the fourth level, the process, risk, and control owners in these organizations more rapidly and easily understand their role and responsibility in closing control gaps, and repairing design flaws and execution errors. Regardless of the risk management culture, expect all who receive bad news to be unhappy and to push back – after all they are only human and resistance is a natural response to bad news.

5. Think about the words that you will use. When in doubt, eliminate all adjectives and adverbs so that your message consists solely of facts. If something wasn't done that should have been, your message should be: This wasn't done x times during the past 3 months (the time period you studied). You don't want to say: This was egregiously not done many times.

6. Be sure to present the context for your observation. If you examined the entire population, say so. If you examined 30 transactions selected from a population of 100,000, you need to say this as well or risk misleading the other person.

7. Think about the feedback you may get from your listeners so that you are prepared to deal with it. Will they react with surprise? Frustration? Anger? Will they question the facts or want to inspect your evidence? Will they willingly accept the facts you present and have questions about suitable corrective action plans? If you get no reaction – no questions, no comments, nothing – seriously question whether your listeners understood your message because this response to bad news is atypical.

8. Prepare for the conversation, so that you don't find yourself delivering the message on the fly. The conversation could get heated and emotional. Sometimes people receiving negative news feel it's unfair. They want to fight back and argue. And as the person delivering the message, you can't let this happen. You need to control yourself in a way that diffuses a potential conflict instead of fueling the fire. You want to prepare for what you're going to say (even potentially scripting out a few opening phrases). You want to prepare for their reaction

– and for your reaction to their reaction. You may even want to rehearse your message so that you are comfortable with it.

9. Pick a time and place when you can be free of distraction. Pick a location that is private and free of interruptions. If the meeting will be virtual, make sure that your background is not distracting to viewers and that you have disabled your pop-ups.

8.4 Tips for Delivering the Message

Deliver bad news early and personally.

Ron Williams

Now that you're prepared to deliver the bad news, keep the following tips in mind:

1. Begin your message with the end or goal in mind. This will help you to be concise. Get right to the point but be as compassionate as you can, given the circumstances. Adopt the tone that you would like to hear if you were in the position of the person who is about to receive the bad news. Announce upfront that you have some unfortunate, disappointing, or disturbing news. The right words? Simple: "I have some unpleasant news."

2. Use "softeners" to open. For example: "I'm sorry to have to tell you…" or "I'm afraid that…" The softeners will enable you to display your empathy.

3. If this is a follow-up communication, summarize the results of each prior conversation or meeting before proceeding to cover "new" material. This helps reestablish rapport and reiterates the major points that have already been discussed or decided.

4. Use plain language. Expressions like "random sampling," "properly accounted for," and "weakness" will trigger suspicion and defensiveness in listeners. Technical terminology will provoke confusion, interruptions, and derailment. As preliminary findings emerge and you begin to draw initial conclusions, informally begin to discuss your results with decision-makers and decision-influencers. Watch their reactions and make appropriate adjustments to your word choice.

5. Cover each topic slowly, using win/win terminology to explain the business impact of each issue or recommendation.

6. Explain the relevancy and impact of each of your points to the business or process objective (i.e., what should be happening) and inherent risk (i.e., undesired and negative outcome).

7. If the news is coming as a shock to your listeners, be prepared for their emotional reaction. Let them vent, if they seem to need to. Do not try to get them to "calm down" or "be reasonable." An emotional response or denial is typical when people are confronted with bad news. Give the other person a few minutes to process your message before proceeding with the rest of it. Don't be surprised if you are asked to repeat the actions you took to determine the nature of your bad news (i.e., the control gap, design flaw, or execution error).

8. If you are concerned that your listeners will have a violent reaction (especially if the issue concerns fraud allegations or unethical conduct), make sure you have provided for your own safety and security. Either have a witness present, or alert security in advance.

9. If appropriate, once the shock has abated, offer the process, risk, or control owners resources they can pursue to correct the situation. If this control gap has occurred in other parts of the company, say this so your listeners realize that others have experienced – and dealt with – the same risk management problems. Suggest possible corrective actions that will address the root cause of the problem.

10. Don't bargain. Don't allow the conversation to become a negotiation when it really can't be one. You are communicating facts about the condition of the internal controls that address the important inherent risks in a process or product. Moreover, you have already identified and assessed the inherent risk's significance and likelihood (whether or not you have assigned a formal rating to this value, you should have conceptualized the risk rating), and this rating should not change as a result of the control evaluation. That is, a high inherent risk

remains a high inherent risk regardless of whether there are any or no control gaps, design flaws, or execution errors. That said, do not be surprised when a process, risk, or control owner wants to reduce the inherent risk rating once an observation or exception is identified.

8.5 Tips to Soften the Blow

While it's never pretty, there are things you can do to soften the blow of bad news. The next time you have to present less-than-favorable information, keep the following tips in mind:

Tailor your presentation appropriately. You wouldn't wear a Hawaiian print shirt to a funeral, so don't use bright colors, cartoons, sound effects, or zany fonts if your PowerPoint presentation contains a series of grim statistics. Stick to a simple background color (or use a standard corporate template) and sans-serif font. Save the transitions and animation effects for a more upbeat presentation.

Don't invite extra spectators. When you schedule a bad-news meeting, it's particularly important to invite only those people necessary to the discussion. For example, when discussing concerns affecting only the Corporate Audit Team, don't invite auditors from other teams. Call a meeting with only the pertinent Corporate Audit Team managers and VPs. Give them the facts, then leave it up to them to disseminate the information to their teams.

Don't be overly dramatic. Okay, some test exceptions and control breakdowns have been identified. While this is disappointing to the area manager, it's not the end of the world. Report the facts, get the manager's agreement on them, and don't exaggerate the impact of your findings.

Include a positive spin. Bad news is always easier to swallow if it's delivered with a positive spin. For example, if you must report that the results of your findings are less than favorable, you'll also want to include some positive news, for example, that local management has already begun to take action... if this is true.

Don't sugarcoat it. On the other hand, be careful not to sugar-coat the information. You have an obligation to share the facts – even if they're alarming or upsetting to others within the organization. After all, it's business. Numbers fall, campaigns fail, employees don't work out, and the economy slumps – people cope with bad news every day. Be forthright, objective, and optimistic – it's the best way to deliver bad news. And, the sooner the bad news is communicated and understood, the sooner corrective action can occur to improve results.

For Skill Practice

1. Imagine that you have some bad news to deliver. How will you prepare?
2. What information do you need to share with your boss and team members?
3. Which constituents need to know?
4. What information do you need to understand their informational needs?
5. How jargon-free is your message?
6. What key points do you want them to take away from your message?

Chapter Summary

- When delivering bad news, remember you didn't create them. Forgive yourself for being the bearer of bad news – you are not causing the distress, the news is. You are conveying facts about a situation.
- Communicate your results including bad news as soon as possible in order to have surprise-free audits or advisory projects. Get in the habit of discussing issues as they come up.
- The sooner you communicate control gaps, design flaws, or control execution errors, the sooner business management can take corrective action - in some cases, even before the audit or project is over. And if the corrective action works as intended you will have contributed to improving your organization's results.

Note

1 The Capability Maturity Model (CMM) is a framework that describes an improvement path from an ad-hoc, immature process to a mature, disciplined process focused on continuous improvement. The CMM defines the state of a process using a common language that is based on the Carnegie Mellon Software Engineering Institute Capability Maturity Model.

My Takeaway Game Plan

My Goal is:

Behaviors I will *start* to achieve my goal...

Behaviors I will *continue* to achieve my goal...

Behaviors I will *stop* to achieve my goal...

Leading and Lagging Indicators – How I'll Measure My Results

9

Ways to Overcome Objections and Resistance

An objection is not a rejection. It is a request for more information.

Brian Tracy

Canadian-American motivational public speaker and author

Before discussing objections and how to handle them, let's take a moment to consider the big picture. What are we trying to accomplish? We want to enable business managers to achieve their business objectives and improve the risk management culture and practices. So, our goal is to reach agreement or closure with business management as soon as possible. And, if we cannot agree, we need to know that we disagree as soon as possible.

9.1 Getting Closure

When I ask participants in my training classes to describe what getting closure means, almost all define it as getting a yes or some type of agreement from their constituents. Actually, this isn't correct. Getting closure (aka closing) means getting a yes or a no from the other person in response to your idea, suggestion, or recommendation.

While it's clear that getting a yes is a desirable outcome; knowing that the other person is opposed to the idea is also helpful. When you get a yes or a no, you know where you stand with the other person. And, your goal is to get a response that enables you to know that the idea, recommendation, or corrective action will or will not occur. Maybe doesn't count. In fact, hearing "maybe" may be the biggest time waster of all. "Maybe" is a stall and I will explain how to deal with it as well as the objections constituents have.

> Getting objections means getting through.
>
> **Anonymous**

9.2 Your Attitude toward Objections

So many of the techniques helpful in dealing with objections come directly from techniques used by sales people that I typically start my classes on how to handle objections by asking the participants to tell me where they would place salespeople on a scale that starts with amoeba (a single-cell life form) at one end of the spectrum and has deities at the other end. Invariably, the participants (who are generally auditors and risk managers) recall negative experiences they have had with product pushers and, based on these experiences, rate all salespeople, including the ones who are professionals, closer to the amoeba end of the spectrum.

You may wonder why I start these training sessions this way. It's simple: if you don't like salespeople, you won't like using the techniques that they use even if these techniques are useful and effective. You'll tune out. And, you'll miss time-tested, reliable ways of handling and resolving objections and pushback.

The techniques in this chapter are ones that professional salespeople – the ones who want to meet the needs of their customers to recreate loyalty and a long-lasting relationship – use. So now you know. But how do you deal with objections?

When someone says no to one of your ideas, what's your reaction? Annoyed? Irked? Piqued? Interested? Curious? Your reaction affects your ability to deal with pushback.

Imagine that you have just made a recommendation and that you receive one of the following responses. Which of them do you like the most and which do you like the least:

Response #1: I like your idea. Let's do it.

Response #2: Sorry, we don't have any available resources to do what you are suggesting.

Response #3: Thanks for sharing your ideas. (*Pause.*) So, what else do we need to discuss today?

When I have posed this situation during a training session nearly everyone (except the most competitive people who thrive on debating everything) chooses Response #1. Let's face it, who doesn't like to hear "yes" and reach a quick agreement? (Of course, there are some skeptics who question a quick win and want to make sure that the agreement is real.)

When I ask participants to name their least preferred response, #3 is always the clear choice. Why? Although Response #2 may sound like your recommendation was turned down and rejected, Response #2 actually gives you several opportunities to continue the conversation. You could ask the other person a couple of questions like:

- Why do you believe additional resources would be needed?
- How do you envision the implementation of the idea? (This vision may be something that is more complicated and time-consuming than what you intended.)
- What type of resources do you think are needed to implement this recommendation?

You could also find out whether the other party would implement the suggestion if resources were available. If the other person likes everything about your idea except the resources required, the two of you could think about ways to implement the idea without needing additional resources. Essentially, Response #2, which seems to be an objection, is really a request for more information or a disguised buying signal. And, if you handle this type of response the right way, your ideas will be accepted more often. More on this in a bit. Now, let's consider Response #3.

On the surface, Response #3 seems innocuous or benign. It may even seem to be a better response than Response #2. But, if you were to receive Response #3, you have no easy way to restart the conversation about your idea. Unlike Response #2, Response #3 shuts down the conversation concerning the suggestion and gives you no easy way to open it up again. Response #3 shuts down the conversation on the topic of your recommendation. If you were to receive this response, you might even experience an awkward pause in the conversation.

My point is that objections are constructive and, more importantly, your reaction to them matters immensely. Objections enable you to identify the aspects of a suggestion that are acceptable and those that need to be adjusted, avoided, or eliminated. Consequently, unless the other party gives you an immediate and resounding positive response to your idea, you should look forward to hearing the other person's objections. Once the pushback is voiced, you can start problem-solving in earnest. Knowing the objections will enable you to come up with viable solutions.

If you don't ask, the answer will always be no.

Nora Roberts
American author

9.3 Using Objections to Your Advantage

An objection is a disguised buying signal. The typical reaction of most people is to become defensive when objections are raised. If that's your immediate reaction when you're on the receiving end of an objection, you're not alone. It's the norm to view objections as negative indicators and roadblocks to your efforts. On the surface, the other person has not accepted your suggestion; you have not received tacit approval to move forward with your idea. Yet, if you reverse the logic, you can actually turn those objections into positives by regarding them as gateways into the other person's thought processes. Objections, if viewed in this positive way, are really just the other person's way of voicing concerns and explaining primary needs. Objections are your constituent's way of opening up to you and really getting to the bottom of what is needed. By encouraging the other person to express the reasons why your idea is unappealing, you can quickly assess the other person's whole package of needs, and address each objection and turn it into something positive.

While some constituents are adept at voicing their needs as needs, others voice their needs as objections. Essentially, it is easier for them to discuss what they don't want rather than to articulate what they do want. Think about it. It's always easier to critique than it is to create. So, accept that the first reaction to your ideas will be critical and expect that response as typical. (Of course, your idea may be accepted immediately, in which case just say "thank you.")

9.4 Stalls versus Objections

Stalls and objections are not the same. If you can't tell the difference, you may be wasting time and missing opportunities to reach a decision concerning ways to improve business practices and processes.

How many times have you heard a constituent say:

- I'd like to think it over.
- I want to review the information you gave me.
- I'll take it under consideration.
- This isn't a good time. Call me next week.

And after you hear this, what do you do? If you say "ok" and make a note to follow up in a week or so you have made a HUGE mistake. You have been stalled and you will waste time following up. More importantly, you have missed an important opportunity to identify the true source of the objection.

An objection is a reason or argument presented in opposition to a point or proposal. A stall is something that prevents a constituent from acting now. A stall signals conflict. The conflict is the constituent's agony of indecision between the desire to act on the recommendation (or deal with the situation in some way) versus feelings of uncertainty and anxiety. When the constituent's desire to make a change is great enough this person will usually agree. A stall normally means the constituent does not have enough reason to agree NOW – this person doesn't sense a need or have the urgency badly enough.

> For change to happen, the value of the change needs to exceed the cost of the status quo.
>
> **Anonymous**

Think about changes you have made. They all required some effort – more effort than remaining with the current situation. Why did you make the change? At some level you realized that making the change would make you happier, better, more efficient, or some other outcome that you wanted more than the status quo. Keep this in mind as you make recommendations or suggestions to others. They will be more willing to accept your ideas if they can immediately appreciate that they will be better off by changing than by retaining the status quo. And, equally important, if they do not perceive any value from your recommendation – or the cost of change exceeds the cost of the status quo, you will receive pushback.

So, what should you do? One of the most undeveloped strategies is to key in on the constituent's positive emotions about your recommendation or the situation. Removing an objection (a negative) can neutralize a block in the decision process. However, that's not enough.

The constituent will agree only when he or she feels a strong positive benefit. Your job is to discover what those benefits are and help the constituent focus on them.

Try to find out the reason the constituent feels he or she might need more time to "think about it." The best way to identify the source of the objection is to ask. You might ask:

- What do you need to think over?
- What is blocking you from going forward?
- What other information will you need before making a decision?
- What other considerations will you want to think about before going ahead?
- What are other concerns you have that we need to talk about?
- What other questions do you have that need to be answered before you feel comfortable making a decision?

When constituents identify their reasons for indecisiveness or reluctance, you have an opportunity to convert the objectionable parts of the recommendation into something appealing and acceptable. If you accept a stall, believing the constituents will agree at a later date, you'll waste time and delay your audit's completion. Once constituents realize they can stall successfully and extend deadlines indefinitely, they will do so every time they face a decision.

9.5 Techniques for Overcoming Objections

Objections occur naturally during the closing process. There are two ways to handle them:

Preventively: This means that during your planning and analysis you anticipate objections and preempt them. Preempting objections means that you state the objection before the other person can express it and you state how this objection can be overcome. One way to preempt objections is to make sure you are talking to the right level of business management – someone who is responsible for achieving the project or process's outcome.

Prescriptively: This means that you counter the objection after the other person has mentioned it. The prescriptive approach can sometimes create the impression that you are defending your position. This impression can undermine the potency of your position – especially if you are unprepared to deal with the objection. In general, it is better to prevent objections than to have to deal with them once the other person has brought them up.

If you start asking questions versus backing off, you will start to eliminate the objection the moment it comes up.

9.6 The Fundamental Rules for Handling Objections

Following are some things to do when dealing with pushback:

- Never tell a constituent, "What you need to understand is…." As an adult, your constituent has free will and doesn't have to listen to you. This message sounds like it would be better coming from a parent than a peer.
- Never allow a constituent to put you on the defensive. Keep in mind that receiving pushback means that the other person heard your message and responded. Okay, so the initial response was not what you wanted but you now have an opportunity to question the person to better understand the source of the objection and overcome it.
- Never let an objection go. Ignoring pushback will not make it go away, nor will it resolve it. Accept that pushback is an ordinary part of the process and move on to figure out its source.
- Always listen – really listen – to the objection. Always acknowledge the objection and then state your point of view. Always be prepared to prove your position with testimonials, reference sources, and corroborative documentation.
- Always remember that objections are a natural part of the audit process. If you are not getting pushback, you are either talking to the wrong person or the other person isn't listening to you or the person hears but doesn't understand what you are talking about.

9.7 How to Overcome Objections Once They Are Raised

Once you hear an objection, consciously tone down your approach immediately. The more you care about an issue, the less likely you are to be on your best behavior. Now, you may think that you don't care about the issue because, after all, it's just work, but you may have invested more than you realize. Let's face it, you have spent some time doing the work that enabled you to identify an issue and then come up with a recommendation. At a minimum, you have pride in your work and want it to be appreciated and valued.

Here are a few steps to take once you receive pushback concerning your point or idea:

- Begin by believing that the other person might have something to say.
- Restate the objection to make sure that you understood what was said. Sometimes what you think is an objection is really a misunderstanding. The restatement also assures the other person that you were listening to what was said.
- Ask clarifying questions to identify the reason for the objection. For example, suppose your constituent said: What you are suggesting would make it impossible for us to do business! Your response could be: What about the idea would make doing business so difficult? Or, you could respond: Really? Why? Ask as many clarifying questions as you need to understand how the other person heard and interpreted your message. Essentially, this step means using a Pull approach instead of a Push. Refer to Chapter 5 for more about this influencing technique.
- Then, just listen carefully to the response to determine the source and cause of the objection.

Address the objection by using one or more of the following approaches:

1. Correcting erroneous beliefs or assumptions.
2. Clarifying the nature and extent of required changes.
3. Reiterating the business risk using different expressions, examples, or war stories.
4. Quantifying or qualifying how the benefits of accepting your position will offset the business risks.

Ask the other person whether you have overcome the objection. If the answer is no, ask what information would overcome the objection. Then seek to provide that information. Be as patient as you can and realize that overcoming objections takes time. It is not something that you can expect to speed through. In fact, you will need to overcome objections at every level of business management, beginning with the control owner and working your way up the corporate ladder. So, you need to be prepared to handle 7–9 objections for each issue as a natural part of the audit. Essentially, you need to be prepared for a marathon, not a sprint.

9.8 Typical Objections and What to Say

If you are being as transparent and open as possible, you should discuss your observations and concerns as soon as possible. Do not wait for the closing or exit conference. (I mentioned this earlier in this chapter.) As soon as you suspect something is wrong, check your work and talk to your manager. Vet the issue within the audit team first and then approach the control performer or owner using the Columbo Detective approach. Ask seemingly ordinary, innocuous questions. Begin by asking the control performer or control owner to review the test work you have performed to make sure you did it correctly. If they agree that your work is correct, then start the root cause analysis: they need to be able to explain how these test results could occur.

Keep in mind that the natural human response to receiving bad news is denial: this isn't happening; this news isn't correct.

Following are some objections your constituents might bring up during an audit, review, or project.

YOUR CONSTITUENT SAYS:	YOU SAY:
Too Little Money: "There's no money in the budget to fund what you are suggesting."	How much do you think it will cost? Or: If there was money in the budget, would you implement this idea? (Be ready for the person to say no. This might be the first of several objections before you reach the root or real one that needs to be addressed. If the response is no, you are being stalled. You will need to switch to a more open questioning approach and ask why.)

YOUR CONSTITUENT SAYS:	YOU SAY:
Too Little Staff: "The Staff is over-committed now."	What do you think staff involvement would be to implement this idea? Or: When is a better time? (Be prepared for the other person to say the staff will be available on the First of Never – another example of a stall or "surface" objection, but not the real or root reason for the pushback.)
Busy Staff Schedule: "These are our peak production periods."	How much staff involvement do you think will be necessary to implement the idea? Or: When is a better time? (But remember what happened before. The answer to this question will let you know whether you are being stalled or whether you have reached the real or root objection.)
The Risk is Not Perceived: "So what? What's the business impact?" (Typically, a response when the auditor or reviewer has not done a good job of describing the inherent risk event and the consequence or when the consequence is hackneyed or inconsequential.)	If you thought a business impact could happen, would you implement the idea? Or: Explain the issue using the Critical Linkage™ as the context. Refer to Chapter 7 – Speaking with Tact, Confidence, and Impact for guidance concerning how to do this.
Denial: "This couldn't happen here." (Typically, a response when a control gap or design flaw exists but no loss or harm has occurred......yet.)	If it did, how would you know? Or: Share a war story about a similar situation.
Negative Impact on Sales: "Your ideas would make it difficult to do business."	What about this idea would cause a problem? Or: Share a war story about how other organizations (similar to the one under review) successfully handled similar situations.
Scapegoating: "It's not up to us; it's the responsibility of <name of another department, company, or person>." (This response typically occurs when the issue is access related and the business manager blames the area that processes or maintains access.)	Who is responsible for the information that is accessed? Or: Who would be responsible if the information was compromised or stolen?
The Residual Risk is Misunderstood: "We are willing to assume that risk."	Who else has agreed to this decision? Or: Where is this decision recorded?

YOUR CONSTITUENT SAYS:	YOU SAY:
Dilettante: "Just because it's in a book (e.g., an industry standard), it doesn't make it right. We are a unique organization (or department, product, process)."	How do you define what good looks like? Or: What rules apply to what you do?
Other Review Results: "We were just audited by <name of group or agency> and they gave us a clean bill of health." Alternate version: We just went through SOX (or MARS, JSOX, etc., testing) and there are no holes in our SOX.	What was the scope of their review?
Status Quo Security: "We've been doing it this way for years without a problem."	If you had a problem, how would you know?
The Unknown: "We don't know what would happen if we make the change."	What are you concerned about? What is the worst thing you could imagine (and would it be worse than incurring this risk)?

9.9 Four Closing Techniques

As we discussed at this chapter's start, closing means getting a yes or a no; maybes indicate stalls and ambivalence. And, while it is never pleasant to hear a turndown, you know where you stand and you can begin your questioning approach to identify the blocks that need to be addressed in order to overcome the objection. Some auditors wait until the exit or closing conference to get agreement on recommendations or business management's planned corrective action. This is a mistake and a time waster. Seek agreement as soon as control gaps, design issues, and execution errors are identified – which may be during while you are planning the audit and setting its scope. Every time you make a suggestion or recommendation, get in the habit of listening carefully to the constituent's response. Is it a yes, a no, or a maybe? The following techniques will make it easier to get a yes or no response from your constituents:

1. **Use Tie-downs** – These are two – or three-word phrases expressed as a question that require the listener to respond by saying "yes" or "no." The answers should be self-evident and affirm your position. This closing technique is most effective when you want to gain incremental support for your ideas. Tie-downs can be used either at the beginning or at the end of a sentence. Tie-downs include: "Do you think?", "Do you

agree?", "Could you?", "Shouldn't it?", and "Isn't it?" For example, "You want to get the most out of your staff, don't you?" or "Do you want to get the most out of your staff?" Never use the same tie-down twice.

Using tie-downs too often can foster a sense of "bullying" and cause the other person to become nonparticipatory and confrontational. In addition, when the other person becomes aware of the technique, the tie-downs lose their effectiveness.

2. **Tell War Stories** – War stories are anecdotes that illustrate and support your point. Use them to underscore key points you are trying to make. Tell no more than 1–2 stories for each point. Make sure that war stories are indicative of general trends and that they serve to focus the listener's attention and support toward your position. War stories represent excellent opportunities to express your position in terms that the listener views as relevant and understandable. Make sure your war stories are true and accurate. For example, you might tell the person you are auditing about another division that experienced a similar control gap, design flaw, or execution error and that they handled it successfully using the approach that you are suggesting. War stories that the other person can verify are most credible and most valuable. When it comes to tough situations, most people like to know that they are not alone and that there is a time-tested fix for the situation they are in.

3. **Reduce It to the Ridiculous** – This technique is effective when people are concerned about the bottom-line budget and the other person's objection centers on implementation costs and budgetary constraints. Many times, falling within budget is the critical and deciding factor. People want their staff to be more effective but they are not always able to rationalize spending the money to make the necessary changes. When using this technique, take the estimated cost of the suggested change and reduce it to a cost per transaction or individual. This approach will reduce the cost to pennies per day.

4. **Be Silent Immediately after the "Ask"** – Once you have posed a closing question (e.g., "So, do you agree to change the work assignments to build in some checks and

balances?"), remain silent and wait for the other person to respond. Learn to tolerate silence. Silence allows the listener to organize his/her thoughts and forces the other person to answer your questions. The next time the other person becomes silent, let silence reign.

For Skill Practice

1. What are the typical objections you face?
2. Are these really objections or just stalls?
3. Should you use a push or a pull strategy to address each one?
4. What are the words you will use to respond to each objection?
5. How will the other person respond to your words?
6. What, if anything, will the other person say to counteract your message?
7. How will you respond?

Chapter Summary

- Welcome objections; don't be afraid of them. A no can be just as meaningful as a yes. Your goal is to get a response that enables you to know whether the other person agrees with the idea, recommendation, or corrective action.
- Objections are your constituent's way of opening up to you. It is the other person's way of explaining primary needs and voicing concerns. When someone disagrees, encourage this person to express why your idea is unappealing. By understanding what the person dislikes, you can begin to come up with options that are more appealing.
- People will agree to act only when they believe they will benefit from doing so. Your job is to discover what those benefits are and communicate them in a way that resonates with the other person.
- The best way to handle objections is preventively, this means that you anticipate the objections and preempt them. It means that you state the objection before the other person can express it and you state how it can be overcome.

- Ask the other person whether you have overcome the objection. If the answer is no, ask what information would overcome the objection and provide it.
- The goal of overcoming objections is to close, meaning getting a yes or a no; a maybe indicates stalls and ambivalence.
- Seek agreement as soon as control gaps, design issues, and execution errors are identified which may be at the start of a project or audit while setting the scope and objectives.
- Remember: overcoming objections is a marathon, not a sprint.

My Takeaway Game Plan

My Goal is:

Behaviors I will *start* to achieve my goal...

Behaviors I will *continue* to achieve my goal...

Behaviors I will *stop* to achieve my goal...

Leading and Lagging Indicators – How I'll Measure My Results

10

MANAGING AND RESOLVING CONFLICTS

Conflict cannot survive without your participation.

Wayne Dyer

Self-development author and speaker

At some point during your career, you will have to deliver bad news. When you do, you might expect the other person to question (read: challenge) your ideas, what you did and how you did it. Why? Because skepticism and pushback are a natural human reaction to bad news. And, if you read Chapter 9 you are now prepared to respond and deal with the other party's objections and pushback.

In fact, if you have taken my advice to heart, you will not only expect the pushback – you will almost look forward to it because you recognize objections for what they truly are: the areas or topics that need to be addressed before the other person agrees with the information you are providing. If you aren't getting pushback after you have described a high-risk situation, a control gap, a control design flaw, or a control execution error, you are either talking to (1) someone who is not responsible for the area, (2) someone who already knows about the problem (which may be due to scarce or insufficient resources) and wants you to report the condition so that senior leadership will take action to correct it, or (3) someone who is not listening to you.

While having the ability to deal with objections is important, it doesn't mean that you will be able to avoid conflict entirely.

10.1 Sources and Symptoms of Organizational Conflict

The potential for organizational conflict is inescapable. Recall typical team formation according to Bruce Tuckman's Stages of Group Development. Initially a group forms, then storms and norms before it performs as a team. Forming and storming are basic, unavoidable

DOI: 10.1201/9781003093978-10

steps in this process. The storming stage occurs before norming (rule-setting) can occur. However, when the group can't progress into the norming step (i.e., cannot come up with ways to fix or avoid problems), conflict can sprout. For example, during the storming stage, group members may become so frustrated by the series of problems they encounter that they become demotivated or specific group members may develop irreconcilable differences and conflict can occur.

Conflict in organizations can exist between individuals in the group, between groups, and between an individual and the group. The causes of organizational conflict can be distilled into three broad areas:

1. Different Missions: It is not unusual for different departments or groups within the same organization to have different ideas and perceptions regarding their group's purpose. These different perceptions can cause conflict. Let me give you an example. Years ago, I worked with a credit card company whose Marketing department was incented based on the number of accounts in the database, regardless of whether the accounts were active (i.e., in use and with a balance) or not. At the same time, those in Credit Underwriting were incented based on the number of active accounts; inactive accounts were viewed as a wasted credit line that could be granted to someone else. Each time a database "cleanup" project was the topic of discussion, both groups disagreed on what to do. Over time, this repeated (and repeated) disagreement developed into "them" versus "us" interactions on other subjects as well.

   Another example comes to mind with a completely different genesis. When I worked with one state government agency, projects that required any time of IT support for implementation would grind to a halt because the head of IT and the head of Operations did not get along (to put it mildly) and engaged in passive aggressive behavior with each other. (Passive aggressive behavior appears tolerant and cooperative on the surface but doesn't deliver on deadlines. The information provided is either incomplete, or in the wrong format, for the wrong period, delivered late...you get the idea. And, when confronted, the person manifesting the passive aggressive behavior apologizes, vows to provide the needed information, and the process repeats itself until either the deadline is blown or the issue is escalated to a level of organizational power that can mandate a resolution. This behavior reminded me of the expression: When elephants fight the only casualties are the ants. In this organization, the employees who reported to the heads of IT and Operations realized that they were the ants in this situation and they wisely kept a low profile and even lower expectations when it came to expecting deliverables from projects that required IT and Operations to collaborate (and nearly all of the important projects required these two individuals to interact).

2. Internal Group Competition: Conflict can occur as a result of internal competition between groups that perform similar functions. For example, the Sales Groups A and B sell the same products but to different markets. Initiation of a sales contest between these two groups can result in either positive, motivating rivalry or potentially hostile conflict, depending on how the contest is managed. If each Sales Group concentrates on making sales within their prescribed target areas, the competition can remain healthy and productive. But, if the pressure to make sales ignites a "win at all costs" mentality, members of Sales Group A may begin to make sales to Sales Group B's targets and account cannibalism can occur. Although the sales members may earn commission, the company as a whole doesn't benefit. This type of conflict can occur in support and control departments like audit departments, as well. In one audit department, conflict existed between the Quality Control department and the rest of the auditors. Those performing the quality control reviews spent all of their time scrutinizing the workpapers, identifying breaches of audit methodology, and providing feedback to the rest of the department. They spent no time actually auditing. When the members of the Quality Assurance Improvement Program (QAIP) team were not scrutinizing the workpapers, they were updating the methodology documentation to "clarify" (read: expand) the documentation

requirements. All of this was occurring at the same time the Chief Audit Executive (CAE) was exhorting all auditors to "make the plan" and do more with less (something that caused several of the auditors to want to reduce the size of the QAIP team). Over time, the auditors began to resent the "constructive comments" from the QAIP team and view the QAIP members as residents in an ivory tower within the audit department. The resentment affected morale and overall performance. While compliance with IIA Standards is important, it shouldn't be the primary or central focus. The ultimate outcome of assurance work is value creation in the form of sustained, measurable improvement in the organization's performance and risk management.

3. Individual Competition: In any organization, career-minded individuals compete for future promotions, raises, status, recognition, and other indices of their organizational stature. Conflict becomes inevitable and destructive whenever an individual in the group:

   a. becomes "obsessed" with acquiring organizational rewards,
   b. repeatedly acts like a dilletante or narcissist (procedures are important – but not for me),
   c. repeatedly disagrees with group decisions, or
   d. repeatedly misses group deadlines (causing the team as a whole to fail to meet its goal).

Notice that all the three causes of conflict require time – one disagreement won't cause a conflict but an undesired and unresolved pattern of behavior repeated over time will.

Each of these causes of conflict thwarts an organization's ability to achieve its goals by wasting time and effort. Unmanaged conflict creates an unproductive work environment, one in which resources are wasted and organizational goals may not be accomplished or may take extra time and resources to achieve.

If an organization has effective monitoring and project management practices in place, the symptoms of organizational conflict will eventually be reported to senior leadership in the form of missed deadlines, unforeseen problems, and delayed results. Consequently, it is better to address the root cause of conflict when it first appears.

When conflict becomes a win-lose contest in our minds; we immediately try to win.

Thomas Crum
A conflict management specialist

10.2   All Disagreements Are Not Conflicts

Many people believe that disagreements and conflicts are the same. Technically, they aren't. Merriam Webster defines "disagreement" as a variance or difference of opinion. Disagreements can be easily resolved and those who disagree can even coexist ("we'll agree to disagree") relatively peacefully. In contrast, conflicts are situations that develop over time in which personalities replace issues. Conflict situations are characterized by a loss of objectivity in one or both parties. This definition has two important components and both need to be in place for a conflict to exist.

The first component is that conflicts occur over time; one or two disagreements does not mean that a conflict exists between two parties. However, if the two parties cannot agree on *anything* no matter how large or small (e.g., meeting times, the order in which to cover specific topics during a meeting, the risk rating of findings), the stage is set for a potential conflict. But, the second component also needs to be present for the stage to be set for conflict: personalities replace the issue. Let me give you an example. Imagine that I see Muffy's phone number pop up on my phone and my immediate reaction is a feeling of irritation and frustration as I wonder just what Muffy wants now. Keep in mind, I have yet to *actually answer the phone.* My entire reaction occurred in a split second simply by *seeing* Muffy's number on my phone (and more importantly, because in the same split second I recalled every tough conversation and disagreement I ever had with Muffy). Since I haven't actually spoken to Muffy yet, I really don't know what she wanted. Maybe she wanted to give me a heads-up on a recent development or maybe she wanted to give me some good news. I won't know until I call Muffy back, but in the meantime my reaction indicates a conflict situation.

Notice in my example that my reaction stems from multiple dealings with Muffy that were difficult. Since it takes "two to tango" and two to disagree, I am responsible for the status of my relationship with Muffy. Maybe I didn't adapt my communication style enough or at all to get on her wavelength. (See Chapter 5 on Influence.) Maybe I didn't understand her needs or provide her with the information she expected when I delivered my message. (See Chapter 7 on Speaking with Tact and Confidence.)

Ideally, the goal is to prevent conflicts from occurring by making informative and accurate presentations and effectively overcoming the other party's objections. Essentially, you want to handle the tough topics very well because these areas are frequently the sources of future conflict. Preventing conflict is preferred to having to deal with it once it has occurred.

10.3   Are We Causing Conflict Unintentionally?

Typically, we think of Information Technology, Information Security, compliance, audit, and risk professionals as people who help others avoid or resolve organizational conflict. However, our communication (what we say as well as what we do not say) may unintentionally trigger disagreements that are repeated over time and become conflicts. Consider the following examples:

- We are interviewing a business manager to identify inherent risk but the other party is thinking about and describing residual risk. It's not surprising that we would have different ratings.
- We may not overtly discuss the inherent risk rating with the constituent until we have completed control operating effectiveness testing or until we issue the report. This delayed communication – one we didn't believe we needed to have – could be a big (read: negative) surprise to the report's reader.
- We assign ratings to our findings, observations, or recommendations yet we don't have defined criteria to measure inherent and residual risk. Effectively, the ratings are subjective and vary from project to project. And, each auditor's ability to explain the rationale for the rating varies – some explanations may be clearer and better rationalized than others. Or, the observations may be rated inconsistently from project to project.
- When discussing test results, we don't mention the number of items in the sample or whether we have used software to test the entire population. We just cite the percentage rate (or number) of errors we identified. Omitting this information

from the initial message could seem disingenuous to the listener.

- We use inflammatory words like "fail" or "lack" when describing situations in which control gaps, design flaws, and execution errors exist in a business process.
- We discuss the usefulness of management monitoring (using the COSO definition) to address a specific risk while talking to an IT professional who is using the same term with a colloquial meaning. No wonder we will draw different conclusions about the control design.

Each of these examples could become chronic miscommunication and the basis for conflict. And, each can be easily and quickly rectified. The sooner we recognize miscommunication and take action, the sooner we can get the relationship back on track and prevent conflict from occurring.

> 10% of conflicts are due to differences in opinion and 90% are due to the wrong tone of voice.
>
> **Anonymous**

Have you ever been in a conversation that takes a topical turn and causes you and others to feel uncomfortable, stressed, and unsure of how to proceed? If the conversation is virtual or in-person, you might notice that people react to the tough topic by becoming consumed with note-taking or averting eye contact by looking anywhere but at the person who has broached the tough topic. The discomfort is sudden and palpable. If this has ever happened to you, you were involved in a crucial conversation and the outcome of these types of exchanges can create or avoid conflict.

Crucial conversations are risky, controversial, and emotional because

- Opinions vary: You think a situation is high-risk and the other person thinks it is low-risk. Or, you think a policy is needed and the other person doesn't.
- Stakes are high: When discussing crucial conversations, reaching mutual agreement is important because both parties' egos and reputations are on the line. In the absence of mutual agreement, potential competition and a win-lose mentality can occur (i.e., the person whose opinion or perspective is

accepted has "won" and the person whose opinion or perspective is rejected has "lost"). Win-lose environments are fertile ground that fosters conflict.

- Emotions run strong: For a conversation to become crucial, one or both parties involved need to believe strongly in their position. Each side is trying to influence the other and by definition, influence requires commitment to one's position or goal (Chapter 5 discusses influence.) Consequently, you or the other person may also feel annoyed, stressed, or frustrated.

People will forget what you said; they will forget what you did. But they will never forget how you made them feel.

Maya Angelou
Poet and civil rights activist

10.4 Handling Crucial Conversations

Any time you need to deliver bad news – or potentially bad news to another person, there's a possibility that the conversation may become crucial. Prevent or preempt the tough conversations by asking yourself the following questions as you prepare to deliver these messages:

- What do I want as an overall outcome?
- What kind of working relationship do I want with the other person?
- How do I need to behave if I really want these results?

Come up with answers to these questions as you plan your message. Clarify what you really want (e.g., I want the other person to acknowledge the performance gap). Then, clarify what you really don't want (e.g., I don't want to have a tense conversation that creates bad feelings and results in no change). Finally, formulate a more complex problem by combining the two answers into an "AND" question that requires more creative and productive solutions (e.g., How can I have a candid conversation with the other person to acknowledge the performance gap AND avoid a tense conversation that creates bad feelings and results in no change). Consider the answers you come up with and plan your messages accordingly.

Sometimes, your best planning efforts are not enough; you may find yourself in a crucial conversation, anyway. When faced with an unexpected crucial conversation, fight the tendency to pretend it didn't happen and overlook it. If you choose to avoid the situation and ignore it, you (and maybe the other person as well) will fume silently and the situation may grow as you replay it in your mind. Also, fight the tendency to replace your goals with ones that will be unproductive in the long run, for example,

- Saving face.
- Avoiding embarrassment.
- Being "right."
- Punishing others.
- Wanting to win.
- Seeking revenge.
- Wanting to remain safe.

These behaviors are forms of avoidance and will hinder your ability to work through the issues with the other party. And, when overused or used at the wrong time, avoidance can exacerbate conflict. Think about it. If you do not let the other party know that you disagree during a status meeting or conversation, how will the person find out? Will you wait until you need to write a report and then deliver the bad news for the first time in a formal format? Bad news does not get better with time….it gets worse.

If you are involved in a conversation that is becoming crucial, you are emotionally involved – otherwise you wouldn't feel uncomfortable – yet you need to decide how you want to handle the situation. You don't want to confront the tough topic and handle it poorly because this will make the situation worse. You also don't want either party to act precipitously and make a decision in haste that they will regret for a long time. Worse, the situation may escalate if you do not handle it well and it becomes a full-blown conflict.

Ideally, you want to be able to continue the discussion openly and candidly, so that both parties arrive at a useful decision. Following are behaviors that will help you steer the conversation and work through the tough topics

- Establish or reestablish mutual purpose (e.g., compliance with regulations, efficiency, quality results, business goal achievement – essentially revisiting the Critical Linkage™).

- Work toward these common goals.
- Create a free exchange and sharing of meaning.
- Get people to feel comfortable to speak out – demonstrate mutual respect.
- Get all the relevant information out in the open.
- Focus on areas of commonalities and agreement.
- Stay goal focused.
- Avoid the "fight or flight" reaction in you and others.

Think your emotions and reactions out. Remember that the only person you can control is yourself. By changing your behavior you will cause a change in the other person.

> Whenever you are in conflict with someone, there is one factor that can make the difference between damaging your relationship or deepening it. That factor is your attitude.
>
> **William James**
> *Philosopher and Psychologist*

10.5 Typical Views on Conflict

How you view disagreements dictates how you react to one. Following are five ways in which people respond to conflict. These behaviors reflect the degree to which we satisfy our own and other people's needs in a conflict. As you read these descriptions, consider how you typically react when you are in a conflict situation.

  Avoid: You dislike disagreement and will go out of your way to avoid it. Your commitment to avoid confrontation can frustrate those who work with you, especially if you are in a leadership position. Decisions on important issues may be made by default because this style places the concerns of others before your own. Nevertheless, this style is useful when other people can solve the conflict more effectively than you, when issues are beyond your control, or when people will benefit from a cooling-off period.

  Compete: You are not afraid to make unpopular decisions or to make your views known. This can cause or lead other people to agree with you (yes men) or to avoid expressing their true opinions (anything for a quiet life). This style focuses on achieving your goals and satisfying your needs, which is fine if your needs and goals are objectively the most important or urgent (e.g., the organization is not addressing the threat or vulnerabilities in mission-critical, high-risk situations). This style is appropriate when quick decisions or unpopular actions are needed.

Acquiesce: When you are in a disagreement, you let your concern for the needs of other people take precedence over your own needs. In conflicts, you are likely to back down. This can mean that your opinions and concerns are not heard. Other people may lose respect for you and see you as a "doormat" to be walked all over. However, this style is useful in situations where the issue is insignificant to you but important to others, or when continued disagreement would potentially harm you or your team.

Negotiate: This style adopts a consensus approach to conflict. You are clear about your opinions and are willing to listen to other people in order to broker agreement. This style promotes harmony and commitment when people have different needs. However, it can take time and effort and is difficult to achieve when other people do not adopt a similar style.

Compromise: This style sits somewhere in the middle of the other four and seeks some expedient, mutually acceptable solution which satisfies some concerns for both parties. You may give more ground than when competing but less that when acquiescing entirely. You may address an issue more directly than when you avoid it but you will not explore it as fully as you would if you were negotiating. This style involves exchanging concessions or seeking a quick middle ground position.

Whenever possible, preventing conflict by dealing effectively with disagreements as they occur and handling the tough topics as they come up in conversation is better than having to deal with a conflict that has occurred. In conflict situations, the parties involved do not trust each other. And, if you have ever lost trust in another person, you know how hard it is to come back from this position and rebuild the relationship.

If you are involved in a conflict, you may be unaware of the condition. Oh, you know you disagree with the person and probably prefer to deal with everyone other than the individual on the opposing side.

Once you are involved in a conflict, your objectivity has been compromised. You will need to seek help from a neutral third party (i.e., someone who is not involved in the situation and who is perceived to be objective and unbiased) to resolve the situation and the resolution may take time.

Depending on the nature of the conflict and the people involved, the third party may be another member of your team or your boss. Or, the third party may be a member of human resources if the situation is between you and a member of your team or a direct report.

An apology is the superglue of life. It can repair just about anything.

Lynn Johnston
A Canadian cartoonist

10.6 Eight-Step Problem Solving Model

Assuming that you are not involved in the disagreement that triggered the conflict, IT, IS, compliance, audit, and risk management professionals can capitalize on their roles and add value as facilitators to enable the parties in conflict to resolve their differences. Regardless of the style you prefer to use when confronted by conflict, the following steps will help you avert conflicts by resolving disagreements and problems as they arise.

1. Tell the person there is a problem and why it bothers you.
2. Let the person respond to the problem.
3. Agree on the problem, if you can.
4. Ask the person to suggest a solution.
5. Respond to the person's idea. Begin with stating what you like about the idea before describing what you don't like.
6. Negotiate until you agree to a resolution.
7. Set a deadline for implementation.
8. Monitor results to make sure the solution works.

For Skill Practice

1. What would you do in the following situations?
   - As part of your review, you ask the constituent to supply what you describe as "standard documentation" to satisfy a

routine audit step (e.g., obtain a copy of the procedural manual). The constituent provides the document; you review it and realize it is incomplete and outdated in certain sections.

Days later, during a status meeting with this constituent, you tell him that the documentation will be an audit point because of its poor quality. The constituent claims you told him originally "even if I found anything, that it wouldn't be written up," and that you essentially tricked him in some way.

- A senior manager in an area you cover is dismissive and condescending because he/she thinks you don't possess enough technical expertise.

2. When faced with conflict, what is your typical reaction? Do you prefer to avoid or confront it?
3. What is the nature of the conflict you typically face? Is it organizational? Is it one team versus another? Is the conflict between two individuals?
4. How do you know when you are in a conversation that it is becoming a crucial one – what are the warning signals or behavioral indicators?
5. How do you handle crucial conversations?

Chapter Summary

- Conflict may still arise no matter how well you handle an objection.
- Organizational conflict comes up during three situations: when groups have different missions, when there is internal group competition, and when individuals compete.
- Fight the tendency to avoid conflict or ignore it. Avoidance can exacerbate conflict when the issue or topic is important. Bad news does not get better with time. Continue the discussion openly and candidly so that both parties can arrive at a useful decision.
- Unmanaged conflict creates an unproductive work environment, one in which resources are wasted and organizational goals may not be accomplished or may take extra time and resources to achieve.

- If an organization has effective monitoring and project management practices in place, the symptoms of organizational conflict will eventually be reported to senior leadership in the form of missed deadlines, unforeseen problems, and delayed results. However, valuable time has been wasted. Consequently, it is better to address the root cause of conflict when it first appears.

My Takeaway Game Plan

My Goal is:

Behaviors I will *start* to achieve my goal...

Behaviors I will *continue* to achieve my goal...

Behaviors I will *stop* to achieve my goal...

Leading and Lagging Indicators – How I'll Measure My Results

11

SPECIALIZED NEGOTIATION SKILLS

Let us never negotiate out of fear but let us never fear to negotiate.

John F. Kennedy

Think of negotiations – what typically comes to mind? Buying a house or car? Resolving a labor dispute? Reaching agreement on contract terms? All of these typical negotiations have one thing in common: two parties with different agendas and objectives are trying to reach an agreement involving limited resources. Those resources are typically money or money related (for example a labor contract may have terms pertaining to the number of vacation or sick days, which intrinsically has a monetary value).

In most of these negotiation examples, the opposing parties will never interact with each other after the deal is closed. Both sides are trying to optimize the result in their favor. Consequently, both sides can "pull out all the stops" and behave as aggressively as they want to reach their goals, knowing that the negotiation is a one-time situation. Think about it. Unless you are a fleet manager responsible for buying vehicles all the time, how often do you buy a car? And, when you buy a car, how many cars do you buy at one time? The typical person buys one car at a time – certainly not a frequency that would create car buying negotiation expertise.

DEFINITIONS OF NEGOTIATION

KEY DEFINITIONS

Negotiation: To confer with another so as to arrive at the settlement of some matter; a means of resolving differences and allocating resources; a process by which two or more parties reach an agreement that is satisfactory to all and that is implemented within agreed time frames.

KEY DEFINITIONS

Negotiating Rationally: Rational negotiations aim to reach the best agreement, not just any agreement. The best agreement is one that maximizes your interests. When you negotiate rationally, you avoid decisions that leave both you and those with whom you negotiate worse off.

When you negotiate rationally, you focus on the one thing you can control: your own behavior.

Typically, the goals of both sides involved in a negotiation are mutually exclusive, which creates the potential for an adversarial, competitive situation. The goal of car buyers is to get the most features at the lowest price. The same is true for those buying real estate. At the same time, the goal of car and real estate sellers is to charge and get paid the most amount of money for the asset.

However, unlike the people involved in real estate, contract, and car buying situations, those involved in internal audit, risk management, and other internal support functions will need to interact and collaborate again and again with the others involved in the negotiations. We cannot afford to use tactics that will burn a relationship bridge that we need to cross repeatedly. Our overarching goal is to improve the risk management culture and processes within the organization.

Consequently, all of the tactics that could be used during a negotiation are not suitable for intraorganizational use. Traditional negotiation ploys and gambits will just create conflict and waste internal resources.

It is not an accident that the topic of negotiation and its use is at the end of this book. Prior to negotiating with anyone concerning risk management practices, you should have already reached agreement with them concerning the process or business objectives, the things that could inherently go wrong, how and why these negative outcomes could happen, and the importance or priority of the inherent risk. You should also have reached agreement on the main ways this risk is managed (i.e., it's avoided, it's internally controlled, it's transferred, it's accepted). If the inherent risk is internally controlled, you should have discussed and reached agreement on the type of control, how it is supposed to work, and whether this is sufficient to bring the level of residual risk to an acceptable level for the organization. Essentially, you will use negotiation skills for a very specific purpose and only after you have discussed the components of the Critical Linkage™ with the business or process owner because the other person needs to be convinced that the inherent risk's consequence is real and relevant to be motivated to come up with a way to reduce the negative risk exposure. Bluntly, if you want to make the best use of time and arrive at useful, lasting corrective action plans, do not negotiate a corrective action plan unless the other person is sold on the risk (i.e., believes the potential inherent risk exists).

> Place a higher priority on discovering what a win looks like for the other person.
>
> **Harvey Robbins**
> *Author and business psychologist*

Negotiation is a complicated communication because it involves all the attributes of a presentation with the unpredictability of a conversation and requires a well-developed vocabulary while keeping one's objectives in mind and anticipating the other party's goals. This is easier said than done. Typical communication behavior is to articulate one's goals – which seems clear-cut from an audit or risk management perspective (e.g., do more of this, enhance that, stop doing this, etc.) – and not consider how the other side may respond or react, which is a big mistake.

Effective negotiation requires comprehensive planning and consistent execution against this plan. Perhaps the most important aspect of negotiation is that it isn't over until the entire deal is done. Just because you got agreement to address one of the issues on your list doesn't mean that you will get agreement on other ones that are important. Although you have reached agreement concerning how some issues will be handled, none of these agreements are final until all of the issues have been discussed and resolved.

11.1 Characteristics of the Ideal Intraorganizational Negotiator

So, if you are going to be an effective negotiator, you need to be:

Patient – Arriving at corrective action plans that address the root cause of control gaps, design flaws, and execution errors or addressing the inherent risks in adopting new technologies, hardware, and software can require a series of meetings and the development of new policies, workflows and approaches.

Persistent – Compromise is often attractive just because it offers an easy way out. Successful negotiators know the key areas of value and sticks to their plan and principles. Moreover, just because business managers or process owners have said "no" once, it does not mean they will keep saying "no." A closed issue can always be reopened. Being too pushy is as damaging as being a push over – so persistence, not insistence, is key. Reiterate the inherent risk's impact on the achievement of the business or process objective – the result that business managers and process owners care about.[1]

A great listener – Research shows that most of us only absorb 20% of what is said to us. In negotiations, that missed 80% is likely to contain crucial information about the other side's tactics and goals. Those who fail to listen, fail to win. If the other party has acknowledged the inherent risk's impact on the business objective, what is preventing this person from agreeing to a corrective action plan? What is the source of the objection? (See Chapter 9 for ways to overcome objections and resistance.)

Observant – In addition to what is said and the rate of speech and tone of voice with which it is said, the other person sends you information in nonverbal ways – but you have to be paying attention and observant to notice it. For example, the way the other person relates to you and how this interaction changes (or doesn't) as the two of you discuss each item of discussion provides insights into what is and isn't important to the other person. Someone who is observant has an advantage.

Flexible – Negotiators must be able to recognize the times when it makes sense to compromise or trade concessions to reach a useful agreement. It is unreasonable to expect the other person to compromise all the time. Concessions, traded at the right time in the meetings, can lead to effective results.

Realistic – A pragmatic approach is crucial. This means knowing what can and cannot be negotiated (e.g., the facts can never be compromised or altered), when to escalate the issue to the next level of management, when to use – and how to counter – negotiating ploys, all the while keeping the whole project or audit in perspective, and being decisive without making assumptions.

Perceptive – Effective negotiators must be able to put themselves into the other person's shoes and display empathy. They are able to understand the other person's personal and professional motivations and any important hidden subjective factors, such as political infighting, which could affect this person's negotiating position.

11.2 The Role of Negotiation in Risk Management

Negotiation is the ability to use exchanges and trade-offs to accomplish objectives while upholding auditing and risk management principles. It requires an understanding of the project or audit objective, methodology, and principles and relies on well-developed communication, listening, conflict resolution, and problem-solving skills, which is why I have waited until the end of the book to discuss this topic. It is the ability to present ideas in a manner that preserves the self-esteem of all parties involved while achieving a predefined goal.

Unlike proficiency in math and science, expertise in negotiation is difficult to assess primarily because it is an intangible ability. Ask someone to add two and two. The answer is finite and definitive, immediately indicating a level of arithmetic ability. Ask someone to negotiate and the likely response is a stream of questions: Why, how, when, etc.?

Some professionals misunderstand the purpose and value of negotiation and perceive it to be an acquiescence or yielding response to pressure. Sometimes, negotiation is viewed as a sugar-coated name for strong-arming others to agree to a particular outcome. Sometimes negotiation is viewed as a mental manipulation, twisting words to achieve a result. None of these view's definitions are correct but these perceptions affect one's willingness to negotiate.

Negotiation is a skill, not a science. Since it is inherently situational, an effective negotiator requires a broad and adaptive range of behavior. The appropriateness of a particular negotiation style or technique considers the issues under discussion as well as the personalities, preferences, and objectives of all those involved. Consequently, negotiation strategies are not one-size-fits-all situations. The specific strategies need to be developed to suit each point under discussion and to appeal to the different personalities involved in the situation.

Negotiation also involves the selective and appropriate use of trade-offs or exchanges. Ultimately, the negotiated agreement must withstand the scrutiny of pragmatism and sound business judgment: did it achieve the desired result without compromising auditing and ethical principles?

While opportunities for negotiation may exist at any point in an audit, the facts (i.e., the findings and the criteria) are never negotiable. You will always report the results of your observations, interviews, and other tests. To do otherwise would be unethical. However, stating just the facts is sometimes not enough to spark corrective action or a comprehensive risk management response.

Yet the following specific audit, risk management, and internal company situations benefit from using negotiation techniques:

1. Setting the start date of a review, audit, or project.
2. Determining an audit or project's scope.
3. Determining the number of staff assigned to the project or audit.
4. Identifying which members of the constituent team will be interviewed to gain an understanding of the process, inherent risks, and controls.
5. Deciding in what order the data collection interviews will occur and how long each interview will last.
6. Prioritizing risk management initiatives.
7. Determining the content and due dates for management of corrective action plans.

11.3 Four Key Indicators to Gauge the Success of a Negotiation

The goal of any negotiation is to arrive at results that are acceptable to everyone involved. The following are four key indicators to gauge the success of a negotiation:

1. All major interests have been met.
2. The critical interests of the other party have been met.
3. The relationship is good. The next negotiation session should be at least as easy as this session was.
4. The outcome is better than any alternative you could develop alone.

If one side believes that it was taken advantage of or received an unfair outcome, this party will feel resentful and look for ways to get out of the agreement. It may also do the least amount of work needed to meet the letter of the agreement, not necessarily its intent. And, worst of all, the next time this party needs to negotiate with you, the experience will be more difficult and competitive, which is the opposite of the desired outcome needed.

By planning well and following this plan during the negotiations, you will increase your ability to meet these criteria and achieve useful results that benefit all involved and your organization as well.

11.4 Guidelines for Planning Effective Negotiations

Negotiation skills are useful in helping business managers or process owners formulate suitable and realistic corrective action plans to address risks and vulnerabilities and increase the likelihood of achieving the business objectives. However, the business manager or process owner has to understand and agree that the inherent risk's impact is serious and its likelihood is plausible. Otherwise, this person will not be interested in discussing remediation. (Refer to Chapters 6, 7, and 8 for ways to facilitate these conversations, speak with confidence and tact, and deliver bad news without engendering bad feelings.) Once the business manager or process owner acknowledges the risk, the following approaches will help you plan your negotiation:

1. Determine your goals as specifically as possible...but remember to keep all your options open. Usually, there is more than one way to get what you want, (i.e., a solution to the root cause

of the control gap, design flaw, or execution error). Essentially, your aim remains firm while your methods for achieving it should remain flexible.

2. Identify the things most important to you and rank them in terms of priority. Identify areas that you feel are vulnerable to attack by the other side. As part of this step, identify who on the business side agreed to the inherent risk's existence and impact on the business or project objective. If no one on the business side has overtly agreed that the inherent risk is a threat to the achievement of the business objective, gaining this agreement is the first order of business. If the business or process owner does not perceive the inherent risk to be compelling, then this person has no reason to negotiate a corrective action plan to correct any control gap, design flaw, or execution error.

3. Prepare, prepare, prepare. Learn all you can about the situation and the other people who will be involved in the negotiation. Find out what is important to them. Use the grapevine. Become adept at managing the information it carries. Cultivate people in the other side's network so that you are aware of current events.

4. Adopt a winning attitude. Be positive, yet emotionally detached, persistent, objective, and professional.

5. Practice by using mental rehearsal. In your mind, rehearse what you will do and say under as many circumstances as you can imagine. If a particular situation stumps you, take time to figure out a response.

6. Consider the business impact as well as possible line and audit management reactions to your message and come up with alternatives.

7. Don't be intimidated or impressed by flowery titles or "experts." Remember that everyone is human.

8. The other person's behavior is motivated by expectations, personality traits, thinking and communication styles. Additionally, communication and thinking styles directly impact the ways in which you and the other person send, receive, and process information during the negotiation

process. Some people are very logical, detail-oriented, and concretely sequential (i.e., agendas and topics are organized based on a methodology like chronology or risk rating), while other people are heuristic thinkers who make associations and conclusions that may appear on the surface to be random. Identify the other person's preferred style early in the audit process so you can adapt and convey your message in a manner that optimizes the other person's buy-in and agreement while upholding auditing and risk management principles.

9. Select the negotiating style that is most appropriate for the situation and the people with whom you will be negotiating. Generally, you will want to use a cooperative negotiating style. However, if the issue involves regulatory compliance, which is traditionally a zero-tolerance area and the other party is resistant to taking corrective action, you might adopt a more unyielding posture when dealing with this specific issue.

When selecting a negotiation style, you have three choices: rigid, adaptive (flexible), or passive. Your choice in style depends on the following factors:

- The importance of the topic or issue under discussion.
- The other person's personality, approach, experience, and negotiating style.
- Your personality and experience.

Since you may need all three styles during one negotiation, you need to be comfortable using all of them, especially if you typically negotiate by yourself.

NEGOTIATING STYLES

Choices in Negotiating Styles

Rigid -------------------------**Adaptive-Flexible** -------------------------**Passive**

As the name implies, the Rigid style is unyielding, unwilling to change, or compromise. Although this may seem like a tough and competitive stance, it is beneficial when you are discussing a very serious situation, literally one that is nonnegotiable (i.e., the proverbial "deal-breaker" that will not allow you to achieve your primary objective). The Rigid style transmits decisiveness, control, and forcefulness. It is useful when the issue is clear-cut, not controversial, or important (e.g., zero-tolerance compliance issues). This style can cause the other person to adopt a Passive style. When over-used or used inappropriately, the Rigid style's results are diminished because the other person accedes without conviction, adopts a passive aggressive posture (i.e., verbally agrees but behaviorally does nothing), and tends not to implement the negotiated outcomes or implements it to the "letter of the law" but not its spirit.

The Adaptive – Flexible style is willing to compromise or exchange concessions on specific points to achieve the objectives. This style is the one many associate with a negotiator's behavior. It enables the other person to contribute to the negotiated outcome, engendering a sense of co-ownership and commitment, along with a desire to implement the outcome. This style requires a lot of give and take between the two sides, which can be very time-consuming. The negotiators on both sides need to have well-developed empathic, listening, and verbal communication skills. The Adaptive-Flexible style is most effective when both sides have compatible goals and values.

The Passive style does not reveal its user's objectives or true feelings concerning the topic under discussion. Essentially, the negotiator remains silent, neither overly agreeing or disagreeing with the point under discussion. This style epitomizes the expression, "If you have nothing good to say, say nothing." This style is helpful when the negotiator needs to buy time or wants to avoid a disagreement or deadlock early in the negotiation process. While this style may seem disingenuous because it enables the other person assume that the silence means that both parties are in agreement, it actually creates an opportunity to continue the negotiation and develop resolutions for the other issues on the agenda. The Passive Style is most effective when the point under discussion is relatively unimportant or when the negotiator wants to move on to another point without agreeing to the point under discussion.

10. Make sure that you have reviewed your negotiation plan with your supervisor and received approval. You want to make sure that you have your manager's support for your approach before you negotiate. Nothing is more embarrassing than having your manager agree with the business or process owner instead of you.

CHECKLIST FOR PRE-NEGOTIATION ACTIVITIES

Have I clearly defined my primary (most important) objectives? These are the outcomes for which I must have agreement and commitment from the other person?

Have I clearly defined my secondary objectives? These are the outcomes that are desirable but not essential.

Have I clearly defined the warning signals that indicate the need to negotiate firmly and overcome the sources of the other person's resistance?

Have I thought about the worst possible consequences of arriving at an outcome that doesn't meet my objectives?

Do I know the background, personality, and experience of the other people with whom I am negotiating and how I will deal with it?

Do I completely understand the issue and its cause?

Do I understand the type of corrective action that is needed to resolve the issue?

Do I understand the Department's historic method of resolving similar issues?

Have I determined what my primary negotiating style will be?

Have I determined what my backup negotiating style will be?

How will I handle delaying tactics and other ploys?

If I am part of a negotiating team, do my teammates and I understand our respective roles?

What is my contingency plan in case my negotiating strategy doesn't work?

11.5 The Importance of Variables

A variable is anything of value to either side. The person with the most variables in a negotiation usually wins because this person has the most options to offer and the most things to trade and exchange to reach an agreement. Ideally, you want to have and be able to offer a variable that the other side perceives as high value but its value to you is low. For example, imagine that you are about to start an audit at month end. The managers of the area you are about to review are usually very busy during the last and first weeks of every month. You could easily move the audit's start date or audit another area; this change will have little or no effect on you and your team. However, being able to move the starting date out a couple of weeks would be of high importance to the other side because it would enable them to wrap up month-end close without additional pressure. In this example, the start date is a variable with low cost to you and high value to the other side.

Following are some other typical variables you could use during a negotiation:

1. The nature and amount of requested information you need all at one time. Technically each report that you request or need could be considered a variable that you could exchange for something from the other side.
2. The date by which you need business manager or process owners to submit the corrective action plan (e.g., moving the due date from a Friday to a Monday without affecting your deadlines).
3. The number of phases that comprise a corrective action plan.
4. The due date for completed corrective action plans.

A negotiator should observe everything. You must be part Sherlock Holmes, part Sigmund Freud.

Victor Kiam
Entrepreneur

TIPS FOR NEGOTIATING CORRECTIVE ACTION PLANS

Points to Remember When Negotiating Corrective Actions

1. Make sure you have "sold" the risk before trying to get agreement on corrective action plans.
2. Be able to express the same concept in several ways until the other person understands your message.
3. Anticipate objections and plan how you will counter them.
4. "Closing" means getting a yes or a no from the other person. "Maybe" is not an acceptable response to a close.

11.6 Tactics for Negotiating Quality Results

Once you have determined your plan, follow it. The following time-tested tactics are useful in person, virtually, and on the phone:

1. Start by setting a pleasant and cooperative tone and the other side will usually respond in kind. Start off slowly, spending time finding common interests and making small talk. Use this time to assess the other person's style so you can adapt to it and empathize.

2. Use the Critical Linkage™ to set the framework for the conversation (i.e., succinctly summarize the business or process objectives, the inherent risks that are the focus of the audit, review, or project, and then the control gaps, design flaws, or execution errors that require attention). If you have been using the Critical Linkage™ as the starting point for all of your conversations, the other person should be nodding in agreement as you explain the context for your meeting. The intent of using the Critical Linkage™ as the starting point is to make sure that you and the other person begin each conversation wanting the same outcome: a well-managed process, one that works without any negative surprises. [2] Then, describe each of the issues or concerns you have identified. Get the other person's agreement on the facts that you have described and ask the other person to suggest approaches to solving the problems and addressing the issues.

3. Avoid using a strict issue-by-issue agenda approach if the other person would like to discuss the topics in a different order because it will make you appear rigid and inflexible. As long as you cover all of the issues, the order shouldn't matter. Besides, you should be familiar with all of the issues and able to discuss any of them in any order.

4. Be sensitive to cultural differences. These cultural differences may be organizational or country-related. Take the time to research the customs and values, so you are prepared and do not unwittingly offend the other person.

5. Never negotiate with anyone who has less authority to make concessions than you do. You don't want to walk away from a meeting thinking that you have reached agreements

concerning the corrective actions or next steps only to find out that the person who outranks the individual you met with is opposed to the agreement. You want to make sure that the other person can honor the agreements and decisions both of you make. Sometimes the easiest way to determine whether a person has the authority to make agreements is to ask: Who else needs to approve the decisions you and I make during this meeting?

6. Find out the other side's deadline, but don't reveal yours. Consider how their deadlines will affect your deliverables, if at all (e.g., has this person scheduled any time off, is this person involved in any other projects or initiatives that could siphon time away from the work they are expected to do for you?). Act as though you have all the time in the world and that deadlines are artificial for you.

7. Create artificial deadlines and a sense of urgency in the other person's mind to keep the project or audit's momentum. Unless you set deadlines for the other person, you may not receive a timely response or get one at all.

8. Remember that all deadlines are artificial. While this tactic may seem to be the opposite of #7, it's not. Deadlines are needed to achieve results, otherwise the work will continue ad infinitum. For example, how many times has an audit or project exceeded its initial budget? And, when it did, what were the consequences? I'm sure the world continued to spin on its axis and the project's end date was pushed out to a new one. Deadlines are educated guesses about how long things should take to accomplish. Audits or projects that have identified serious control gaps, design flaws, or execution errors typically take longer to complete than those with no or low-risk findings. Why? Because there's more to talk about with the business or process owner. And, developing corrective action plans for high-risk findings can be more complex and involved. Do not let your drive to meet your deadlines overshadow the need to arrive at a useful corrective action plan, one that will address the root cause of the issue.

9. Unless you have a good reason to trust the other side, don't. Remain cautious and professionally skeptical at all times. Be wary of the other side's assurances that everything will be all right. Make sure you have documented who will do what, by when to address the situation.

10. Listen actively during the negotiation. Encourage the other side to talk by using open-ended probing questions and by saying "Uh huh," "I see," and other fillers.

11. Use the other side's objections to support your own position. (See Chapter 9 – Overcoming Objections and Resistance.) For example, having made an offer, listen to the other side's objections: it's too complicated, too expensive, too time-consuming, etc. Ask the other side to expand on the criticism of your proposal (i.e., why do they think the corrective action will be too complicated, expensive, or time-consuming?). Mentally record the reasons for the objection. Once the other side has finished expounding on the criticisms, state that you understand the nature of the other side's objections and, in fact, have already considered them in your planning. Use each objection to present a positive aspect of the corrective action.

12. Learn to "call the behavior." If the other side uses an unfair tactic, bring it out into the open and discuss it. For example, if the other side is playing "good cop, bad cop," let them know that you recognize the game. Or, if the other side is playing hardball and threatening you to "take it or leave it," counter this behavior by saying, "That's not good negotiating – What is your objective?"

13. Monitor your emotions. Stay calm and open-minded during the negotiation. Your emotional outlook will cloud your judgment and affect your perception.

14. Use language that most closely resembles that which will be used in the project or audit report. Begin by reviewing the finding and determining if the other person understands its consequence on the achievement of the business objective. If not, you need to convince the other person of the importance of the finding (i.e., make sure that they understand the risk) before you can negotiate any corrective action.

15. Keep your voice level and even. Speak clearly, slowly, and confidently.

16. Negotiate specifics, not generalities.

17. Listen carefully and remember to restate what you have heard to make sure that your understanding is correct.

18. Remember to adjust your tone of voice, word choice, and negotiating style to accommodate the needs and hot buttons of the other people involved.

Never allow a person to tell you no who doesn't have the power to say yes.

Eleanor Roosevelt

11.7 Four Negotiation DON'TS

When negotiating, the details matter. You do not want to undercut your position and start the negotiation with a suboptimized solution. To maintain your perspective, avoid the following mistakes:

1. Don't enter into a negotiation with artificially high demands hoping to spur a fast compromise borne of haggling. I have worked with people who always ask for twice as much as they need, expecting the other side to refuse to meet the initial request. So, each time these folks are involved in a negotiation they inflate their request. What they don't realize is that the other side recognizes this ploy and perceives all requests as unrealistic – even when they may be accurate. Instead of exaggerating what's needed to correct the problem, take the time to set and express reasonable demands. Discuss the other side's reactions, concerns, and objections. Fast haggling usually leaves everyone dissatisfied.

2. Don't express disapproval too quickly. Things have a way of changing, especially when you are dealing with details: what is unacceptable on one day can become acceptable next week. Additionally, your disapproval can be interpreted as a form of uncooperativeness by the other side, creating resistance in him or her.

3. Don't try to handle the toughest issues first. Start with minor issues which are relatively easy to negotiate, thereby building a relationship and creating some momentum. When I explain

this point in training, it seems counterintuitive to some because we are taught as professionals to value time and not waste it, which typically means starting with the most important topic. When negotiating, however, we don't want to risk getting dead-locked during our first conversation, which is something that could happen if we start with the toughest topic first. We also don't want to start our negotiation by having to set aside the first issue we discuss, which is something else that could happen if we start with the toughest issue first. Consequently, it's better to start with some other issues, reach agreement on them, and create some traction for those involved in the negotiation. This way, when the going gets tough as it will when the more significant issues are discussed, both parties can remind each other that they have a history of reaching mutually beneficial agreements.

4. Don't assume. If you act as if an assumption is a fact, you will be stuck with that premise and have to act accordingly.

11.8 Five Outlooks That Lead to Poor Negotiated Results

1. Stubbornness: Escalating your commitment to your initial course of action, even when it is no longer the most beneficial choice and other options are possible.

2. Win/lose attitude: Assuming that there is a direct correlation between your gain and the other party's expense, opportunities for trade-offs that lead to mutual gain are ignored or never considered.

3. No empathy: Failing to consider the situation from the other party's perspective. Critical data concerning the other party's conditions may be overlooked.

4. Susceptibility: Allowing the manner in which information is presented to overly influence your thinking and reactions. This behavior is the opposite of professional skepticism.

5. Selective perception: Anchoring your negotiation strategies to irrelevant information and assuming that initial offers are unalterable.

11.9 Techniques for Handling Special Negotiation Circumstances

11.9.1 For Telephone Negotiations

1. Compared to face-to-face negotiations, telephone negotiations are much shorter, more competitive, and more formal. Therefore, you need to be prepared to use very clear and highly rational arguments to gain added strength. Since you have no visual cues on the phone, pay particular attention to changes in the other person's rate of speech and use of silence to gain insights concerning the issues or aspects of the issues that may be either important or problematic to the other person. If you are not sure of the other person's views on a topic (i.e., the person's response is neutral or hard to interpret), be sure to ask. Do not make assumptions or interpretations.

2. Never negotiate on the phone unless you initiate the call and are prepared to talk details. If you receive a call and you are unprepared to negotiate, say, "Sorry, I can't talk right now. What's a good time to call you back?" You want to have all the information you need to reach a firm agreement. During negotiations, the details are important and you don't want to risk making a mistake.

3. After each telephone call, write an email confirming the contents of your conversation and send it to the other side. If the other side offers to write a confirmation email, suggest that you both write one and then compare notes.

11.9.2 For Long-Term Negotiations

If you regularly negotiate with the same person, vary your communication style. For example, if you are usually very quick to come to the point, spend time chitchatting. If you like to follow a precise agenda, deviate from it. Change venues. Pick different meeting times and places. You do not want to become predictable; you want to keep the exchanges with the other person interesting.

THE RED PEN

My business was about five years old at the time and I was at my desk working diligently on a project for a client when the phone rang.

"The Whole Person Project, this is Ann speaking, how can I help you?", I chirped into the phone as I turned my attention toward the caller. It was Gonzo, a potential client. He had received my proposal for training services and had just finished reviewing it.

"I wanted to let you know that I look forward to working with you on this project," he said. "I liked everything I read in your proposal. There are just a couple of minor things that we need to talk about before we get started."

Hearing these words, I was so excited at the prospect of starting a new project that I grabbed the first pen I could lay my hands on as I scrambled to locate and print out a copy of the proposal. (Okay, I'm old-fashioned – I like to take handwritten notes.) It was a red pen.

"I'm sure we can work things out," I told Gonzo confidently. At that point, I had no idea what the minor things were that he wanted to discuss but it didn't matter because he had already said the magic words: "I liked the proposal and want to work together."

"What changes are you thinking about?", I asked, figuring the changes would be minor and this call would be brief.

"Oh, nothing major….for example, the proposal says that the design can accommodate 12 people and we have 16 on our team. Would we be able to have 16 people instead of 12?"

"Sure," I replied quickly, scribbling that edit on my copy of the proposal as I cradled the phone between my shoulder and ear."Ok. So, when would you like to schedule the training?" I asked, mistakenly thinking that this change was the only minor thing Gonzo wanted to talk about.

"Just one more thing," Gonzo said," could we reallocate the time during the first day?"

"Of course, what would you like?", I replied compliantly. And so it went. After each "minor" request, I thought we were done – but we weren't.

Twenty minutes later, the call ended. Among the minor changes Gonzo wanted were a couple of additional topics, which effectively changed the program design.

In retrospect, I realize how skillful Gonzo was. He created an unconscious bias by describing his desired changes as "minor," which lowered expectations in my mind. He also brought up the "minor" issues in a random order instead of walking through the document page by page, so I didn't realize how many changes there were, especially since I was inveigled by the prospect of working together.

By the end of the conversation with Gonzo, each page was nearly completely covered in red ink. When I realized that my initial proposal was transformed by all of Gonzo's edits, I offered to revise and resubmit a new proposal – with a new price to cover the additional work.

Thank God I had grabbed a red pen. Had I used a pencil, I might not have realized just how many changes I agreed to make. That red pen saved me from making a big mistake.

11.10 Negotiation Tricks and Gambits

When you think of negotiations you may also think of tricks and gambits that the opposing use as both sides look to satisfy their objectives. During traditional negotiations between parties who work for different organizations, buyers may understate the amount of money they have to spend. Sellers may use glowing terms to describe the item for sale. Both sides may limit the information they communicate to each other in an attempt to keep things simple.

As I mentioned earlier, since you and the other party both work for the same organization, these traditional tricks are a waste of time. More importantly, they can damage a relationship that needs to endure because the two of you will likely have to work together again and again.

Nonetheless, some people approach intraorganizational negotiations with a competitive style and they might have a few tricks or ploys on their agenda.

Following are some typical tricks and gambits and how to counteract them.

11.10.1 Negotiating Ploy 1 – The Nibble

You are providing the process owner a summary of the issues that were identified this week:

You: Here's a draft of the issues that we identified this week. We were testing user access and, based on the test results, access for three employees who left the company was never revoked and we couldn't locate support for five changes in access rights that we made for other employees.

Network Access Manager: That's not bad. In fact, that's better than I thought. I'd just like to read the draft issues while you are here. Hmmmm, I'd just like a little wordsmithing.

You: Sure, what did you have in mind?

Thirty minutes later you are still "wordsmithing" with this person. So, what's happening here? This person is using a technique called the Nibble. The lesson here? Never say yes too quickly when the other side makes a suggestion. It encourages nibbling.

11.10.2 Negotiating Ploy 2 – The Flinch

Another ploy is the Flinch. Let's use the same situation as before:

Auditor: Here's a draft of the issues that we identified this week. We were testing user access and, based on the test results, access for three employees who left the company was never revoked and we couldn't locate support for five changes in access rights that we made for other employees.

Business Manager <*Looking shocked and recoiling in horror*>: What!!?? There's an issue with access??!! Eight exceptions?? That can't be right! Did you look at the right reports?

Auditor <*surprised and unbalanced by the emotional response*>: Well, I can double check the workpapers.

> **Business Manager** <still *looking shocked and recoiling in horror*>: Yes. You need to do that. Let's set this point aside until you double-check your work.

The principle of flinching says that you should visibly or audibly react whenever a proposal is made to you because people are watching for your reaction. The "Flinch" is intended to lower the other party's expectations or throw the other person off-balance.

If the other person flinches at your message, be sure to resist the temptation to make a concession or agree to a delay.

11.10.3 Negotiating Ploy 3 – The Higher Authority

Imagine that you are once again discussing recently identified issues with a business manager.

You <finishing a description of the issues identified during testing>: So those are the issues that we identified. What are your thoughts about how to correct these situations?

> **Business Manager:** Thanks for telling me about the issues, but I'm not in a position to make any changes. I don't own this operation.

Have you ever been in a situation like this? Now, perhaps this manager can't negotiate a corrective action plan, or perhaps he can. This manager is using the Higher Authority ploy. Here's how to counter it:

Business Manager: Thanks for telling me about the issues, but I'm not in a position to make any changes. I don't own this operation.

> **You:** OK....so who could authorize a change?

That's a very effective counter gambit. Find out who can make a decision, and then ask to speak to that person.

11.10.4 Negotiating Ploy 4 – The Bottom Line

Let's imagine that you are discussing ideas to improve the way risks are managed in a process:

You: As you can see, we have summarized our observations and ideas for you, and I hope that this gives you a good sense of how you could improve risk management performance in this process.

> **Business or Process Owner** <*speaking in a matter-of-fact tone*>: Well, I really appreciate all the time you've taken to make these recommendations and all the work you've put in, but what you are proposing really is the "Rolls Royce" solution. It looks very complete – but also very expensive – and frankly more than we have budgeted. (*Business or process owner acts like the conversation on this topic is over.*) But to be open-minded..... what's the least we need to do to address this situation?

So, what's happening here? The business or process owner's behavior initially leads you to believe that all of the ideas are turned down. In essence, you have "lost." But then, this person gives you a flicker of hope.... "what's the least that's needed." This ploy targets the typical response to loss aversion which is to limit the loss.

Counter this ploy by reminding the business or process owner of the exposure's consequence on the business objective and the need to implement a corrective action based on its ability to address the root cause of the issue, not just its cost. Ask the business or process owner to suggest ways to address the exposure.

11.10.5 Negotiating Ploy 5 – Good Guy/Bad Guy

Let's go back to the scenario in which the auditor is discussing recently identified issues with the process owner. This time, one of the process owner's direct reports is also in the conversation. We join the scene as the Process Owner says to the auditor:

Process Owner <*speaking loudly and in a slightly belligerent tone*>: Look I'm sorry, I'm not going to waste any more time on this. I've got another meeting to go to. I don't think your corrective action requirements are realistic. Goodbye.
<*With this he gets up and walks out, slamming the door behind him.*>

Process Owner's Direct Report <*Looking slightly chagrined and speaking in an apologetic tone*>: I'm sorry, he gets that way sometimes. He's so difficult to deal with and I'd really like to see this audit wrapped up. Hey, I've got an idea. Why don't you let me see what I can do for you with him?

Auditor: Well, what do you think you can get him to go along with?

Have you ever been placed in this position? If you were the auditor here, and if you were not a skilled negotiator and didn't understand what was happening, you might find yourself asking the Process Owner's Direct Report to negotiate with the Process Owner on your behalf, and he or she is not even in your team!

The best way of dealing with this ploy is to call the behavior and simply tell them that you see that it's just a ploy. There's a saying about ploys: a ploy perceived is no ploy at all!

11.10.6 Negotiating Ploy 6 – The Set-Aside

Imagine a videoconference in which the Process Owner is talking to the auditor about corrective action plans. The meeting has just started and the Process Owner begins with:

Process Owner <*speaking in a confident, matter-of-fact tone*>: Our software doesn't have the feature-functionality to do what you're describing, so there's no point in discussing this any further.

Auditor: But the situation is a risk that needs to be fixed.

Now if the auditor is not careful, this negotiation will reach an impasse and stall even before it has begun; before sufficient momentum has developed; before a relationship has been established; before enough time has been invested; and before all of the factors have been considered. An inexperienced negotiator will either give a concession – possibly unnecessarily – or lose the whole negotiation before it even starts.

So, what could this auditor say?

Process Owner <*speaking in a confident, matter-of-fact tone*>: Our software doesn't have the feature-functionality to do what you're describing, so there's no point in discussing this any further.

> **Auditor:** Let's just set that aside for a moment and let's discuss the other issues, OK?

By temporarily setting the topic aside, the auditor keeps the communication channels open and prevents the meeting from stalling before it even gets started.

11.10.7 Negotiating Ploy 7 – Personal Attacks

If you have ever been on the receiving end of one of the following remarks (or something similar), you have been personally attacked:

1. Unlike you, my team and I live in the real world.
2. If you were responsible for a front-line, core business function, you would understand.

A personal attack may be made on purpose to put you off-balance and make you emotional. Remember, we are creatures of emotion and when we are emotional, we sometimes say, do, or agree to things which in a calm rational state of mind, we would never have considered.

The counter tactic is to simply remain unemotional and detached. Don't take it personally.

11.10.8 Negotiating Ploy 8 – Precedents

This is where the person with whom you are negotiating says something like:

- But why is this audit rated "Unsatisfactory?" I know for a fact that the western region received a "Needs Improvement" rating and we operate the same way they do.
- Why is this an issue this year? You audited us last year and didn't cite this and our process hasn't changed.
- We were audited by <name of external auditor> and they gave us a clean opinion.

In other words, they are claiming that there is a precedent here – a previous case. Sometimes, that will stop even the most skilled negotiator in his or her tracks. The counter gambit is to insist on the uniqueness of the case in hand. You need to be prepared to rationalize and justify your explanation, for example:

- Then was then, now is now. The circumstances are entirely different.
- The audit or project scope was different.
- The items tested were different.
- The testing approach was different.

11.11 Avoiding Deadlocks in Negotiation

Before making any offers, concessions, or counteroffers assess the person with whom you are negotiating. Is the person with whom you're dealing empowered to say yes – not just no? If not, make sure you have the right people at the table to save time. Organizationally, where one sits definitely determines what one sees. If you are discussing a corrective action plan with a control owner, this person will not have insight into the total available budget or resources that could be involved in implementation. This person can, however, say no to your suggestions or recommendations. In this case, you would do better to involve the process or risk owner in the corrective action conversations. These people, by virtue of their higher-level organizational role will be in a better position to make agreements concerning resource allocation and due dates.

As a general rule, never give something without getting something in return. Otherwise, you will be negotiating against yourself. When you concede or in some other way reduce what you are asking for without getting something in return, you are letting the other side know that what you initially asked for you never thought you would get. You essentially are training the other side to simply wait silently until you get too uncomfortable and reduce the ask. This is not a productive habit.

Despite your best efforts, you may find yourself at or approaching a deadlock during your negotiation. If this is the case, any of the following techniques may get the conversation going again on a productive plane.

- Leave the point that is creating the impasse and work on the other points on which may be easier to resolve. This may put the deadlock into a different perspective.
- Change your "Negotiator." Bring in a new person. This individual could be another team member; he or she doesn't have to be your boss.
- Change the competitive atmosphere that inherently is associated with deadlocks to a cooperative atmosphere by taking the stance of the "Problem Solver."
- Bring in other people who have the technical or specialized knowledge to identify alternative solutions.
- Always leave yourself some room to maneuver, so that alternatives can be explored.
- Look at the deadlock from the other parties' viewpoint. They may have backed themselves into a corner they can't get out of and now have no room to maneuver. If this is the case, you must offer them a way out to get discussions moving again.
- Change the specifications within the proposed offer (e.g., create phases for corrective action implementation, describe different resource requirements, suggest different timing of phases).
- Go off the record (e.g., "Strictly off the record, what is the problem?").

- Wherever possible, let the other person suggest the way out of the deadlock. If the other person suggests it, this person is invested in the solution. As long as this suggestion addresses the root cause of the problem it doesn't matter who thought of it.

Don't bargain yourself down before you get to the table.

Carol Frohlinger
author and speaker

11.12 Tactics for Making Offers and Counteroffers

Frohlinger's advice is particularly important to keep in mind during negotiations. Her advice is very helpful when trying to determine when to escalate the conversation and when to offer concessions and make counteroffers.

One of the challenges during a negotiation is knowing when to concede or compromise. Following are some guidelines for making the right decision:

1. Never concede on the facts. Period.
2. Watch your anchors. Many factors influence the initial position people take when negotiating. The initial position act as an anchor and affect each side's perception of what outcomes are possible. An anchor is typically based on whatever information is handy or strategic. This information may be relevant, irrelevant, accurate, or erroneous. An example of an anchor is the listing price of a building or the perceived cost of a corrective action plan. Anchors inhibit people from negotiating rationally. Additionally, final agreements in negotiations are more strongly influenced by initial offers (the anchors), than by the subsequent concessionary behavior of the other party.
3. Don't legitimize an unacceptable initial offer by making a counteroffer. Know enough about the issues to be able to recognize an unrealistic anchor.
4. Never criticize or reject the other side's offer out of hand – unless the initial offer is absolutely unacceptable. When faced with an unacceptable offer, walk away from it (politely), and

end the negotiation. Prepare to escalate the issue to a more senior management level.

5. Don't give up something without getting something in return.

6. Remember that an offer is not the final outcome; you can make a counteroffer.

7. Make concessions only as necessary and always with an explanation as to why you are willing to concede. Avoid making a large concession early in the negotiation.

8. Use the following statements to encourage the other side to make concessions:

   • Where do we go from here?
   • What are we really talking about here?
   • What can you do for us on that?
   • There's got to be another way.
   • You're not giving me anything on this.
   • That would be tough for us. Real tough.

The key point is to trade or exchange concessions rather than to make concessions without getting something back for each concession. When exploring concessions, be sure to use the word "If:"

   • If I do this for you, will you do this for me?
   • If the control could be accomplished without adding to staff, would you do it?

By using the word "if," you indicate that you want to achieve a "WIN/ WIN" solution. You would like to offer the other side something in return for getting something that you require.

Of all the skills we've discussed, negotiation is the most demanding because you need to continually maintain an awareness of the other party's position strategically and tactically vis-à-vis your own.

At this point, word choice really matters as does the ability to be able to deliver the same message in a variety of ways. Essentially, you need to leverage all of the skills required of you at earlier points in the audit or project: executive presence, influence, speaking with confidence and tact, dealing with objections and resistance....and arrive at an agreement that addresses the root cause of the issue.

The success of a negotiation depends on your ability to execute the plan and remain focused and unaffected by whatever ploys or gambits the other side attempts.

For Skill Practice

1. Think about the characteristics of effective intraorganization negotiators. How many of these traits do you have? Which ones are your strengths? Which ones do you need to develop or enhance?
2. Think about the outcomes of your past three negotiations. What would you do the same? What would you do differently?
3. What is your typical negotiating style? What negotiating style in others creates problems for you? How will you adjust to overcome these problems?
4. Think about an upcoming negotiation for a current audit or project. What variables do you have to trade? What variables does the other side have that would be valuable to you?
5. Think about recent negotiations you have had. What tricks or ploys did the other person use? Which ploys did you use?

Chapter Summary

- When negotiating with a constituent, keep in mind that the overarching goal is to improve the risk management culture and processes within the organization.
- Don't try to negotiate unless the other person agrees that the potential inherent risk exists and agrees that this risk is an important threat to achieving the business objectives.
- An effective negotiator is patient, persistent, a great listener, observant, flexible, realistic, and perceptive.
- Effective negotiation achieves the desired result without compromising auditing and ethical principles.
- Use the Critical Linkage™ as a starting point for all of your conversations. This will enable you and the other person to begin each conversation wanting the same outcome: a well-managed process; one that works without any negative surprises.

- Does the person with whom you're dealing have the power to say yes and not just no? If not, make sure you have the right people – the decision-makers – at the table to save time.

Notes

1 If you are already in the habit of using the Critical Linkage™ as the framework for conversations about risks and controls, you understand why it is important to get overt business manager and process owner agreement concerning the inherent risks that are integral to your audit or project. By securing this agreement as early as possible during the audit or project (like the planning phase), you are in a terrific position during corrective action plan negotiation to remind the other person of the prior agreement concerning the inherent risk's negative impact on the business objective.

2 Using the Critical Linkage™ has a been a theme throughout this book. If it is not a habit that you practice, start immediately. It will save you time in the long run and make it much easier to make your points concerning ways to improve risk management practices.

My Takeaway Game Plan

My Goal is:

Behaviors I will *start* to achieve my goal...

Behaviors I will *continue* to achieve my goal...

Behaviors I will *stop* to achieve my goal...

Leading and Lagging Indicators – How I'll Measure My Results

12
WHEN TO LET GO AND MOVE ON

One of the hardest things in life is deciding whether to give up or to try harder.

Anonymous

In each of the preceding chapters, I've implied that if you work hard and demonstrate each of the behaviors I've described you'll achieve your goal and get your way.

This isn't true. No one gets others to agree 100% of the time. There will be times when....

- You make a request and receive a noncommittal answer or worse, get turned down.
- You make a recommendation and receive a stall (e.g., we need to think about it) or pushback (e.g., we don't have the money available to act on your recommendation or we don't agree that the risk is high) instead of agreement.
- You disagree with how the other party wants to handle a situation. The other party wants to wait and see what happens or study the situation a bit more and you feel that immediate action is needed. Or, the other person wants to implement a new technology or launch a new product and you don't see evidence that the inherent risks in this plan have been considered. Or, worse, the other party thinks that the inherent risk has been considered and wants to "assume the risk." Or, worse than that, the other party has already implemented the new technology and you found out about it several weeks after implementation because the other party didn't see the need to involve you in "business decision-making."

DOI: 10.1201/9781003093978-12

- Your priorities and values differ from the other person's. For example, you are extremely conservative and the other person believes that risk taking always leads to or equates to rewards (e.g., whoever gets to market first will acquire the largest market share or competitive advantage).
- You have to work with someone that irritates you and gets on your nerves. Your personal styles may clash. For example, you are attentive to details and the other person is unaware they exist. Or, you are very other-directed, choosing your words with care and anticipating the other person's reaction. In contrast, the other person focuses exclusively on getting results without considering or acknowledging the human effort needed to get the job or project done; the human effort is incidental – results are the only thing that matter.
- You think you have done a good job and the other person either doesn't appreciate it or worse... thinks your work product could have been better.

When these things happen once in a while, it is relatively easy to shake off the disappointment or view the situation as an unfortunate incident or an oversight. After all, everyone's ideas get turned down at some point. Instead of simply accepting the turndown or rejection, you may figure out an alternative approach or rethink and reword your request or recommendation so that the other party agrees to it. But now imagine that every or almost every one of your ideas gets turned down.

Similarly, if your work is critiqued occasionally, this situation would be ordinary and acceptable. But now imagine that your work product never seems to be able to please the other person. Over time you would feel frustrated and demoralized.

And, at some point, you will work on a project and discover that your style or value system radically differs from those demonstrated by the business person responsible for the project. If this happens once in a while, you can flex and deal with it. But now, imagine that this happens on every project. Bridging these differences will start to seem like a full-time job, leaving you with little energy to deal with the project work.

When these disagreements happen on a recurring basis, it is more than an oversight or a mistake. It's a sign that you and others in the organization have irreconcilable differences in values, risk tolerances, and perhaps even ethics. How many times can you accept an apology for the same mistake before you realize that "mistake" will keep happening?

The most precious thing that we all have with us is time.

Steve Jobs

12.1 Dead End Signals

One of the premises of influence is that once people make a decision – even if it's wrong or silly – they believe that they need to stick with it because they like to be consistent. And they use prior decisions as a benchmark for future ones.

If you are in a situation in which the other party has made a decision that, in your opinion, should not have been made, it will be virtually impossible for you to get the other person to reverse this decision. To countermand a decision, the other person would have to admit making a mistake – something that most people are loathe to do because they perceive it as a sign of weakness, especially in a business setting. Once a person who outranks you in the organization makes a decision that differs from your idea or recommendation, you may have reached a dead end on this topic for the foreseeable future.

If you find yourself in a situation in which an important decision needs to be made, don't push for a decision if you're not positive that the decision will go your way. It's better to wait. Use the wait time to figure out which arguments will motivate and persuade the other party. Refer to the tactics in Chapter 5 on Influence and Chapter 9 on Handling Objections and Pushback.

Never give up on something that you can't go a day without thinking about.

Winston Churchill

12.2 When to Persevere and When to Let Go

Churchill's quote gets to the heart of when to cede and when to persevere: if the situation is very important to you, then you persevere. But be careful that your motivation is not simply misplaced competitive energy. Every issue, every recommendation, every situation cannot and should not be one that you need to "win." All business situations are not equally important or equally risky.

Following are some factors that can help you determine whether to persevere or let go. Consider the answers to the following questions as a way to assemble the context or "Big Picture" for the issue or situation you need to address.

1. Begin by understanding what the issue or situation means to you as a person and a professional. Does it affect a core value of yours? Is it unethical? Is it illegal? Is it a preference but not a requirement? Is it integral to goal achievement? So, if the issue or situation affects a routine, habit, or preference, you may want to compromise to reach a workable solution. But, if the issue involves a core value, ethics, or something illegal, pull out all the stops and stick to your position. Use every method at your disposal to convince the other side. Ultimately, though, if you continue to face resistance, walking away may be the only option you have left.

2. Consider who is involved. What is your relationship to these people? Do they report to you? Do you report to them? Are you peers? How influential are those involved? What types of decisions have they made or influenced recently? Pay particular attention to the answers to the last question because, although you may have no connection to these people (i.e., you were not involved in the decisions they made), you do not want to underestimate their power and influence over others. Think about the nature of the relationships these people have with you and with their peers. Try to identify any internal networks or external alliances or connections that exist. Determine whether you or they are more influential within the organization. Recall the reasons they made past decisions

and analyze this information to gain insights regarding the types of arguments that motivate them to act and enable them to persuade others. Do they have a different:

- risk appetite? For example, some people view regulatory compliance issues as zero-tolerance situations while others ponder the likelihood that noncompliance will be identified and fined.
- set of priorities? For some, being the first to market is a priority while others prefer time-tested solutions. Neither approach is empirically correct; these positions represent core values.
- set of experiences? Some have been in the same (or similar) jobs their entire careers. While others have worked for an array of employers in a variety of industries. Some have never been in managerial roles and are unfamiliar with the unique challenges associated with managing and motivating the work efforts of others in order to achieve targeted results.
- set of incentives? Some are used to having "at risk" compensation in which their performance directly affects the amount of their income. Others receive the same salary whether or not they achieve targeted results.
- level of responsibility or accountability or authority? Where one sits determines what one sees. The higher up in an organization one is, the less one is familiar with the details associated with transaction processing. This is a natural phenomenon and accounts for differences in process, risk, and control owners' perspectives on inherent and control risk in a specific process or function.

3. What's the risk or priority involved? Does the situation have strategic importance? Is it regulatory or zero-tolerance in nature? How many transactions or dollars are involved? To what extent does the situation or issue affect customers? How many locations or employees are affected? You may think a situation is mission critical or high-risk, but others don't or vice versa.

BE CAREFUL WHAT YOU ASK FOR

A financial institution needed to fill the leadership role in the internal audit department, an opening created when the incumbent retired. The search committee thought carefully about what they wanted: someone who was up to speed on internal auditing and aware of the best auditing practices. Their search was successful and they hired Gonzo, who was a card-carrying member of the IIA and ISACA and who had earned several designations. Within 2 years Gonzo was gone. Why?

Once hired, Gonzo set about making his mandate for change a reality. He studied the audit methodology he inherited and saw opportunities to introduce risk-based approaches. So, he began overhauling the existing audit methodology to make it truly inherent risk-based at the annual audit planning level as well as during audit execution. He had plans to implement continuous auditing and introduce data analytics. What he didn't count on was the cultural intransigence he encountered at the Audit Committee and Executive levels. Gonzo was so focused on acting on the mandate to create change, it never occurred to him to consider the organizational risk management culture. Had he used the Internal Control Maturity Model (based on the Carnegie Mellon Capabilities Model), he would have realized that he was working in a risk management culture that was far from optimized. In fact, internal audit as a function was viewed more as the organizational watchdog, than the trusted advisor with a seat at the executive decision-making table.

Gonzo's situation was a classic case of "be careful what you ask for because you might get it." When the Audit Committee members and Executives expressed the mandate, they never anticipated the types of change Gonzo would want to implement, which was the root of the problem. Gonzo's recommendations for change were perceived as radical and unnecessary. After a couple of years of being thwarted at every turn, Gonzo got tired of the frustration and left.

4. What kind of precedent does the situation set? The more of a precedent, the more likely people will be against it. Giving the issue a rest (i.e., setting it aside), creates a cooling off period during which additional information can be collected and studied. After some time has passed, you can reapproach the topic, if needed. One of our clients had no interest in virtual meetings or training before the COVID pandemic. Although each member of the team was equipped with a state-of-the-art laptop, the team as a whole preferred group-live sessions when meeting with constituents and participating in training sessions. The team members felt self-conscious on camera and weren't comfortable using the virtual meeting platforms. Sixty days after the pandemic hit, this situation changed completely. Team members, forced to meet virtually, adopted the new behaviors needed to convene and facilitate virtual meetings and moved beyond their history of in-person sessions. Okay, so this example is extreme in that it took a pandemic to change the team members' behavior. Sometimes a big behavioral change can be achieved simply by modifying an incentive compensation plan or having the CEO or Board Chair announce a new policy or performance expectation.

Once you have answered these questions, mentally step back, and consider the aggregated information as objectively as you can.

Begin by assessing the quantitative data you have. Have similar decisions or actions occurred? What were the recorded results? Facts can be very persuasive, especially if your corporate culture values analysis and data-based decision-making, and the data is clear-cut. Unfortunately, when one needs to make decisions about new products, new technology, or new ideas, reliable data that is free of conscious bias is hard to find.

Then acknowledge your role within the organization and realistically assess the power you have a result of your organizational role and the influence you wield as a result of your personality and skill. You may quickly realize that:

• You are outnumbered and even though you may have a valid point, your voice is drowned out by many others (or a vocal few) who feel differently than you do.

- You don't have enough organizational clout and the decision is not yours to make or countermand.
- You have irreconcilable differences in values, which is probably the toughest of these three circumstances.

Any of these conclusions are signals that it is time to let go if they happen on a fairly frequent basis or whenever an important or urgent issue is under consideration.

Under the best of circumstances – like when you are hired to make change happen – trying to affect corporate culture single-handedly is a challenging, long-term undertaking that requires 18–36 months to be viewed by employees as a real, change initiative and 5–7 years for the change to become part of the organizational culture. If you were not hired as a change agent, creating organizational change is very difficult. For example, if you work for an executive team and board that prides itself on being conservative in every way, recommending that this company install the latest technology will trigger resistance. Typically, in a culture like this being an early adopter is not a good thing or a desired outcome. This culture prefers to wait and see how other companies fare before adopting the technology even if this means that they will be in a "me too" competitive position.

Imagine that you really believed (and had data to show) that adopting this new technology was critically and strategically important. In fact, its adoption would be strategically important. When the situation is important to you or your values or ethics (like decisions that involve risk management practices, especially those that involve accepting or avoiding risk), you may initially accept a turndown but will bring up the situation again at a future date. You may use every tactic you know to communicate your message and influence the other person's thinking. You may carefully listen to the other person's concerns, demonstrating the most sympathetic problem-solving behavior you can as you work to identify the sources of stalls and overcome objections.

Sometimes, none of these tactics will work. This may only happen once or twice in your career. But it can happen. And when it does, knowing when to drop the subject, when to cede, and when to let go (i.e., stop) is an important part of communicating. It is also a sign of emotional intelligence.

If you have to drop something or cede a point, it is not necessarily your fault. When the student is ready, the teacher will appear. Your audience might not be ready for the teacher and you just need to bide your time.

If you repeatedly find yourself ceding points or shelving plans – especially in areas that are of great importance to you professionally or personally, you need to find a new place to work – one with a better cultural fit.

For Skill Practice

1. What projects or initiatives that require approval or permission from your boss or a committee have been on your to-do list for more than 6 months? For each one, think about the actions you have taken to:

   • Communicate the benefits.
   • Persuade others to take action.
   • Overcome resistance and objections.
   • Reduce or eliminate conflict.

2. How important (strategically and tactically) is each project to you?
3. How important (strategically and tactically) is each project to your department or organization?
4. What other actions can you take to move each initiative or project forward?
5. Is it time to let go and move on?

Chapter Summary

   • You won't always get your way or accomplish what you set out to do. That's OK. Everyone wins some and loses some.
   • If you find yourself in a situation in which an important decision needs to be made, don't push for a decision if you're not positive that decision will go your way.

   • If you repeatedly find yourself ceding points in areas that are important to you, consider letting go and starting anew someplace else.

My Takeaway Game Plan

My Goal is:

Behaviors I will *start* to achieve my goal...

Behaviors I will *continue* to achieve my goal...

Behaviors I will *stop* to achieve my goal...

Leading and Lagging Indicators – How I'll Measure My Results

Bibliography

Bazerman, Max H. 1992. *Negotiating Rationally*. Edited by Margaret Neale. New York: The Free Press.

Berne, Eric. 1964. *Games People Play*. New York: Grove Press.

Bolton, Dorothy G., and Robert Bolton. 1996. *People Styles at Work: Making Bad Relationships Good and Good Relationships Better*. New York: AMACOM.

Carnegie, Dale. 1936. *How to Win Friends and Influence People*. New York: Simon & Schuster.

Covey, Stephen R. 1989. *The 7 Habits of Highly Effective People*. New York: Free Press.

Duhigg, Charles. 2012. *The Power of Habit: Why We Do What We Do in Life and Business*. New York: Random House Publishing Group.

Gray, John. 1992. *Men Are from Mars, Women Are from Venus: The Classic Guide to Understanding the Opposite Sex*. New York: HarperCollins.

Green, Charles, David, H. Maister, and Robert Galford. 2012. *The Trusted Advisor*. New York: Simon and Schuster.

Hill, Napoleon. 1937. *Think and Grow Rich*. New York: The Ralston Society.

Johnson, Spencer. 1998. *Who Moved My Cheese?* New York: G. P. Putnam's Sons.

Kerry Patterson, Al Switzler, Joseph Grenny, Ron McMillan. 2011. *Crucial Conversations: Tools for Talking When Stakes Are High*. McGraw-Hill Professional Publishing.

Laborde, Genie Z. 1987. *Influencing with Integrity*. Palo Alto: Syntony Publishing.

Ruiz, Miguel Don. 1997. *The Four Agreements: A Practical Guide to Personal Freedom*. Amber-Allen Publishing.

Sedler, Michael D. 2003. *When to Speak Up and When To Shut Up*. Revell.

Warren, Rick. 2002. *The Purpose Driven Life: What on Earth Am I Here For?* Grand Rapids: Zondervan.

Index

Printed in the United States
by Baker & Taylor Publisher Services